BREAKFAST WITH GOD

Quiet Moments with God

Breakfast with God
ISBN: 979-8-88898-118-4 - *Paperback*
ISBN: 979-8-88898-119-1 - *Hardcover*
ISBN: 979-8-88898-120-7 - *Ebook*

Copyright © 2024 by Honor Books
Racine, WI

Cover Design by Faille Schmitz
Manuscript prepared by W B. Freeman Concepts. Inc..
Tulsa, Oklahoma.

Eat your Breakfast!

Breakfast is the most important meal of the day.
Don't leave home without breakfast.
A good breakfast will star with von the entire day.

These phrases and others like them have become well known in our culture, but they aren't just Moms advice anymore! Scientists and doctors have spent millions of dollars to discover what moms have known all along.

However, even more important than a naturally nutritious breakfast is a spiritually nutritious breakfast. Proverbs 31:15 says the virtuous woman rises early to get spiritual food for her household. David said in Psalm 63:1: *"O God, You are my God; Early will I seek You."*

Jesus once said to His disciples, "I have food to eat of which you do not know," then He explained, "My food is to do the will of Him who sent Me, and to finish His work." (See John 4:32, 34 NKJV.) Jesus was saying that He was motivated and energized by walking in obedience to the Father and doing His will. His life flowed from the "inside-out." The same must be true for those of us who seek to follow in His footsteps.

When we spend the first part of our day in the Word of God, prayer, meditation, and praise and worship, we acquire an inner strength and energy that adds vitality to our entire day. This "food for the soul" is truly food that the world does not know about, that prepares us to do the Lord's will. Regardless of where our day may take us or the situations we may encounter, we have a renewed mind to think the thoughts of God, to feel His heartbeat, and to say and do what Jesus would say and do.

After having *Breakfast with God*, you will be prepared to face whatever the day may bring—and end the day with less stress and frustration. God promises that if we seek His kingdom first, all other things will be added to us. (See Matthew 6:33.) When you make your relationship with the Lord your top priority, you are setting yourself up for blessings all day!

Like the First Morning

His compassions fail not. They are new every morning.
LAMENTATIONS 3:22-23 NKJV

What a joy it must have been for the first man and woman to awaken in the morning just after their creation!

Before them lay a beautiful garden without blemish, a harmonious creation without turmoil, an orderly environment without so much as a weed or thorn. Most wonderful of all, they freely walked and talked with the Lord in the cool of the day. Wouldn't you love to experience that glorious state of being for one morning! Eleanor Farjeon must have felt the same elation when she penned the words to her now internationally famous hymn:

"Morning has broken like the first morning;
Blackbird has spoken like the first bird.
Praise for the singing! Praise for the Morning!
Praise for them, springing fresh from the Word!

Sweet the rain's new fall sunlit from heaven,
Like the first dew-fall on the first grass.
Praise for the sweetness of the wet garden,
Spring in completeness where his feet pass.

Mine is the sunlight! Mine is the morning
Born of the one light Eden saw play!
Praise with elation, praise every morning,
God's recreation of the new day!"[1]

While we may not awaken to a perfect, pristine world in our natural bodies, we *can* awaken to a "brand-new day" in our minds and hearts. We can walk and talk with the Lord all day long. Each day the Lord presents to His beloved children wondrous possibilities to explore with Him.

Let us always remember that He is the *Creator and our loving Father*. No matter what state we find ourselves in. He can create something new in us, for us, and through us. What cause for praise! His next act of creation is waiting to unfold as we yield our life to Him this morning and throughout our day!

The Sunrise Travelers

The children of Israel . . . journeyed from . . . the wilderness .
. . toward the sunrising.
NUMBERS 21:10-11 KJV

When Moses led the children of Israel out of Egypt, the people immediately experienced great joy upon being delivered from bondage. However, as they traveled through the wilderness toward the promised land, fear of the unknown would often take hold of their hearts. The following excerpt by Louise Haskins, taken from *Traveling Toward Sunrise*, captures the essence of how all of us press on into unknown territory by simply trusting God:

"These travelers were time's valiant great hearts. They were journeying on the star road making their way through an inspiring land, a desert waste upheld by hope of a glorious new day, a tomorrow morning, when night with its darkness and shadows would be left far behind.

"Travelers whose hopes were fixed on what was before and beyond: men of faith who followed the gleam loyally, right through to the very end: road-makers, presenting an

unparalleled example of courage and bravery; men of vision, always looking ahead, never behind. "What an inspiring, challenging thought as we . . . begin our journey, traveling toward sunrise. Let us begin by filling the air with songs of rejoicing, with songs not sighs, for we are wayfarers of the infinite, traveling to the land where dawns are begotten and glory has its dwelling place, where life begins, not ends, and where there is eternal springtime.

"And I said to the man who stood at the gate of the year. 'Give me light that I may tread safely into the unknown!'

"And he replied: 'Go out into the darkness and put your hand into the Hand of God: That shall be to you better than light and safer than a known way' So I went forth, and finding the Hand of God. trod gladly into the night.

"And He led me toward the hills and the breaking of the day in the lone East."[2]

As you read this, you may be facing tremendous opportunities or overwhelming difficulties. In either case, put your hand into God's hand and walk with Him. Let Him give you comfort and wisdom as you move toward your promised land.

First Cup

In the morning my prayer comes before you.
PSALM 88:13 NKJV

Many people wouldn't dream of starting their day without a cup of coffee. They count on that "first cup of the day" to wake them up and get them going.

There are others who have discovered an even more potent day-starter: first-thing-in-the-morning prayer.

For some, this is a prayer voiced to God before getting out of bed. For others, it is a planned time of prayer between getting dressed and leaving for work. For still others, it is a commitment to get to work half an hour early to spend quiet, focused time in prayer before the workday begins.

Henry Ward Beecher, one of the most notable preachers of the last century, had this to say about starting the day with prayer:

"In the morning, prayer is the key that opens to us the treasure of God's mercies and blessings. The first act of the

soul in early morning should be a draught at the heavenly fountain. It will sweeten the taste for the day.

". . . And if you tarry long so sweetly at the throne, you will come out of the closet as the high priest of Israel came from the awful ministry at the altar of incense, suffused all over with the heavenly fragrance of that communion."[3]

A popular song in Christian groups several years ago said, "Fill my cup. Lord; I lift it up, Lord. Come and quench this thirsting of my soul. Bread of heaven, feed me till I want no more; Fill my cup, fill it up and make me whole."[4]

Morning prayer is a time to have your cup filled to overflowing with peace. Then, as you have contact with other people at home and at work, you can pour that same peace into them. And the good news is—unlimited free refills are readily available any time your cup becomes empty throughout the day!

———————————————————

Today's Sure Thing

The steps of a good man are ordered by the Lord.
PSALM 37:23 NKJV

In his book for children, *The Chance World*, Henry Drummond describes a place in which nothing is predictable. The sun may rise, or it may not. The sun might suddenly appear at any hour, or the moon might rise instead of the sun. When children are born in Drummonds fantasy world, they might have one head or a dozen heads, and their head or heads may not be positioned between their shoulders.

If one jumps into the air in the "chance world," it is impossible to predict whether the person will ever come down again. That he came down yesterday is no guarantee he will come down the next time. Gravity and all the other natural laws change from hour to hour.

Today, a child's body might be so light it is impossible for her to descend from a chair to the floor. Tomorrow, the child might descend with such force, she falls through all three levels of a three-story house and lands near the center of the earth.

In the final analysis, *The Chance World* is a frightening world. While most people enjoy a certain amount of spontaneity in their lives, they enjoy life more when it is lived against a backdrop of predictability, surety, and trustworthiness.

The Scriptures promise us that the Lord changes not. He is the same yesterday, today, and forever. (See Hebrews 13:8.) Furthermore, His natural laws do not change unless He authorizes their change for the good of His people. His commandments do not change. His promises to us are *sure* promises. We can know with certainty, "the steps of a good man *are ordered* by the Lord."

The Lord may have some surprises for you today. They are a part of His ongoing creation in your life. But His surprises are always custom-designed for you on the rock-solid foundation of His love. It is always His desire that you experience the highest and best in your life. You can count on Him!

Share the Secret

I have learned the secret of being content.
PHILIPPIANS 4:12-13

A woman named Frances once knew a young person at church named Debbie. Debbie always seemed effervescent and happy, although Frances knew she had faced struggles in her life. Her long-awaited marriage had quickly ended in divorce. She had struggled to get a grip on her single life. She hadn't chosen it, but she decided she would live it with utmost enjoyment and satisfaction. Debbie was active in Sunday school, in the choir, as a leader of the junior high girls' group, and in the church renewal movement.

Frances enjoyed knowing Debbie. Debbie's whole face seemed to smile and she always greeted Frances with a hug. One day she asked Debbie, "How is it that you are always so happy—you have so much energy, and you never seem to get down?"

With her eyes smiling, Debbie said, "I know the secret!"

"What secret is that? What are you talking about?" Frances asked.

Debbie replied. "I'll tell you all about it, but you have to promise to share the 'secret' with others."

Frances agreed. "Okay, now what is it?"

"The secret is this: I have learned there is little I can do in my life that will make me truly happy. I must depend on God to make me happy and meet my needs. When a need arises in my life, I have to trust God to supply according to His riches. I have learned most of the time I don't need half of what I think I do. He has never let me down. Since I learned that secret—I am happy."

Frances' first thought was, *That's too simple!* But upon reflecting over her own life she recalled how she thought a bigger house would make her happy—but it didn't! She thought a better-paying job would make her happy—but it hadn't. When did she realize her greatest happiness? Sitting on the floor with her grandchildren, eating pizza and watching a movie—a simple gift from God.

Debbie knew the secret, Frances learned the secret, and now you know it too!

———————————————

Do Your Best

*And it will come about that whoever calls on the name of the
Lord will be delivered.*
JOEL 2:32 NASB

D o you ever feel inadequate? Unworthy?
Most of us do from time to time. And we
all know people whom we *think* are too
successful to have those same feelings.

Martin Luther, the sixteenth-century German
preacher and Bible scholar who initiated the Protestant
Reformation, sounds like the type of man who would
be eminently sure of himself. Any man who would
dare to publicly question the theology of his church —
in a time when it could cost him his life — could not be
a man who had doubts about himself. Or could he?

In truth, Luther spent his early years obsessed by
his presumed unworthiness. He periodically fasted and
mistreated his body in an attempt to "earn" God's
favor. On a pilgrimage to Rome, he climbed the Steps
of Pilate on his knees, kissing each step. He wrote later
that in those years he was constantly confessing his
sins to God, yet he never felt he had done enough.

One day while reading the book of Romans, Luther realized he could not earn his salvation. The Bible says we *receive* salvation, we do not earn it. (See Romans 4:13-14.) Those verses of Scripture liberated Luther, radically changing his opinion that it was his works which made him worthy of God's grace.

He recognized Jesus Christ had already done all the "earning" necessary for his salvation. He simply needed to receive what Jesus had done—that He had paid the price for his sin on the cross—by faith.

On days when we fall Hat on our faces in failure or just feel low, we need to remind ourselves that our mistakes are not the end of the world. Our inadequacy is not our doom. Our salvation doesn't depend on how well we manage to color inside the lines!

Perfection may be our aim, but when we realize we haven't arrived there, we need to relax and turn to the Lord, saying, "Forgive me for what I have done, and for what I have left undone. I trust You to be my Savior, my Deliverer, my Hope, and my Perfection." He is and He always will be!

The Morning Sacrifice

Their duty was . . . to stand every morning to thank and praise the Lord.
1 CHRONICLES 23:28,30 NKJV

The Levites were never given the option to skip morning devotions. They were *commanded* to keep the morning sacrifice every day, without exception. As part of the morning ritual in the Temple, the high priest had these three duties:

1.   *to trim the lamps, making sure each oil cup of the menorah had sufficient oil and that the wicks were properly positioned,*
2.   *to burn sweet incense on the incense altar.*
3.   *and to burn the fat of the "peace" offerings.*

Once a week, as part of the morning ritual, the priest replaced the "shewbread" that was on constant display before the Lord.

The priest performed these functions in silent worship, wearing a highly symbolic vestment. As he worked, the only sound was the light tinkling of the bells on the hem of his garment.

This ancient ritual may seem strange and of little meaning to us today, but one great lesson we can draw from it is this: the morning sacrifice involved *all* of the senses and the mind. The priest stood before the Lord with his identity clearly displayed; he stood before the Lord for examination.

His sacrifices touched upon all aspects of his humanity: the lamps symbolized his need for light— the ability to see with spiritual eyes. The incense was a picture of his need to dwell in an atmosphere infused with Gods holy presence. The peace offerings were a sign of his need for peace with God and his fellow man. And the "shewbread" demonstrated his need for daily provision, which only the Lord could provide.

This was a ceremony that, in its silence, spoke clearly: "We need You. Without You, we have no life, no wholeness, no meaning."

We may not have a ritual to follow in our morning devotional times, but we must come before the Lord with the same spirit of dependency and obedience. The day ahead of us is not ours. Our lives belong to God. (See 1 Corinthians 6:20.)

Everything we need. He will supply. The day is His, even as we are His.

The First Sunrise Service

I will sing and give praise. Awake, my glory! Awake, lute and harp! I will awaken the dawn.
PSALM 57:7-8 NKJV

The year was 1909, and the place was Mount Roubidoux in California. In the valley at the foot of the mountain was Mission Inn. Here, staying as a guest, was Jacob Riis, the famous social crusader and father of slum clearance in New York.

As Riis looked up at the crest of Mount Roubidoux, he caught a vision. At the inns evening song service, he shared his thoughts with Frank Miller, the proprietor, and the assembled guests:

"I see in the days to come an annual pilgrimage – call it what you will – winding its way up the steps of Mount Roubidoux, climbing ever higher toward the cross that crowns the summit, where the bell peals out its message of peace on earth and good will to men, and gathering there to sing the old songs that go straight to the hearts of men and women."

Riis spoke as a prophet, but even he could never have dreamed how soon his words would come true. The next Sunday was Easter, and Miller decided to make its observance memorable. He invited one hundred of his guests and friends (Riis had left by then) to climb Roubidoux and hail the breaking of the holy day with a simple but impressive service.

In the light of that Easter dawn, the first sunrise service on record was held by those one hundred "pilgrims." Today Easter sunrise services are a yearly tradition for Christians around the world. While not everyone can greet this holy day from the top of a mountain, just praising God while watching the first rays of sun appear over the horizon can make one's spirit rise. Even when the day is overcast, there is something wonderful about watching God's beams of light break through the clouds to warm the world.

There is no need to wait for Easter, however. You can make any day a holy day by dedicating it to the Lord. Why not set your alarm so you can enjoy your own private "sunrise service" tomorrow morning!

Talk with the Creator

Wisdom begins with respect for the Lord; those who obey his orders have good understanding.
PSALM 111:10 NCV

"There is literally nothing that I have ever wanted to do, that I asked the blessed Creator to help me do, that I have not been able to accomplish. It's all very simple if one knows how to talk with the Creator. It is simply seeking the Lord and finding him." These are the words of the great scientist, George Washington Carver, the American botanist who literally rebuilt the Southern agricultural economy after the Civil War.

Born a slave, Carver eventually became head of the Agriculture Department at Tuskegee Institute in Alabama. He developed more than three hundred uses for the peanut and dozens of products from the sweet potato and the soy bean. Much of Carver's research was conducted in his laboratory, which he called "God's Little Workshop."

"No books are ever brought in here," he said, "and what is the need of books? Here I talk to the little peanut and it reveals its secrets to me. I lean upon the 29th verse of the first chapter of Genesis. 'And God said. Behold I have given you every herb bearing seed which is upon the lace of all the earth, and every tree in the which is the fruit of a tree yielding seed; to you it shall be for meat.'"

Carver had a habit of seeking the Lord early in the morning. He rose at four o'clock everyday and went into the woods to talk to God. He said, "There He gives me my orders for the day. I gather specimens and listen to what God has to say to me. Alter my morning's talk with God I go into my laboratory and begin to carry out His wishes for the day."[5]

You can begin each day asking your Creator what He would have you do that day and how He would have you do it! If you are facing a challenge, God can reveal a new perspective. If you need inspiration, God can stir you up. If you feel you are in a dead-end situation, God can show you His way out.

Seek your Creator today! He desires your fellowship and He wants to give you the answers you need.

Straight Ahead

It is God who arms me with strength and makes my way
perfect.
2 SAMUEL 22:33

T he sun is barely up and that annoying alarm clock is blaring in your ear. Groggily you reach over and fumble around until you hit the snooze button. *Just a few more minutes, you think, and then I can get up and face the day.*

The alarm sounds again. You know you can't put it off any longer. It's time to face the inevitable. It's time to wrestle another day to the ground.

After a couple of cups of coffee, your brain is finally humming. Now the question is which of today's tasks should you tackle first? Before you begin your work, you might seek inspiration from this prayer, written by Jacob Boehme, a German shoemaker who was born more than 400 years ago:

"Rule over me this day, O God, leading me on the path of righteousness. Put your Word in my mind and your Truth in my heart, that this day I neither think nor feel anything except w hat is good and honest. Protect me from

all lies and falsehood, helping me to discern deception wherever I meet it. Let my eves always look straight ahead on the road you wish me to tread, that I might not he tempted by any distraction. And make my eves pure, that no false desires may he awakened within me."[6]

A day without distractions, focused only on the important.

A day viewed through pure eyes.

A day marked by goodness and honesty.

A day of clear direction and no deception.

A day without falsehood and lies.

A day in which God's Word rules our minds and His truth reigns in our hearts.

Now that's a day worth getting up for! That's a day worth embracing fully, from the first second.

———————————————

Morning People

God called the light Day, and the darkness He called Night.
GENESIS 1:5 NKJV

God made both the day and the night and He called both of them good. It seems God also made "morning people," who have their greatest energy level in the morning, and "night people" who are most productive in the late hours. Let's look at some of the joys of being a morning person.

God promised the children of Israel they would see the glory of the Lord in the morning (Exodus 16:7). This promise came to them when they were hungry and in need of bread to eat. God supplied manna every morning until they reached the promised land. Like the children of Israel, we too can see the glory of the Lord when we seek Him in His Word. Each morning He provides the nourishment we need for the day.

Another blessing of morning lime is it often brings an end to suffering and sadness (Psalm 30:5). Each day brings us a new opportunity to seek God for a fresh perspective on the problems and needs in our lives.

When we give every minute and every circumstance of each day to the Lord, we can expect to see His light dawning throughout our day.

There are many examples in Scripture about people who rose early to meet God or to be about doing God's will, among them Abraham, Moses, Joshua, Gideon, Job, and even Jesus. The Gospels tell us that Jesus went at dawn to teach the people who gathered in the temple courts.

The most glorious event of Christianity—the Resurrection—occurred in the early morning. Each morning we can celebrate Jesus' Resurrection as we watch the light of the day dispel the darkness of night.

———————————————

The Greatest Artist Paints Daily

Have you not known? Have you not heard? The everlasting God, the Lord, the Creator of the ends of the earth, neither faints nor is weary.
ISAIAH 40:28 NKJV

Peter the Great ruled from a palace filled with some of the most exquisite works of art produced in the world up to that lime. Yet, when he pondered a sunrise, he wondered how men could be so foolish not to rise every morning to behold one of the most glorious sights in the universe.

"They delight," he said, "in gazing on a picture, the trifling work of a mortal, and at the same time neglect one painted by the hand of the Deity Himself. For my part, I am for making my life as long as I can, and therefore sleep as little as possible."

Peter the Greats observation tells us something about his general outlook on life. Not only did he know true beauty when he beheld it, but he believed that rising early every day to drink in the beauty of

Gods marvelous work of art would actually add days to his life.

That concept is not so far-fetched if we consider what psychologists have told us about relieving stress. You can alleviate stress by getting up earlier and spending some quiet time enjoying a sunrise!

Chicago produce dealer, John Cooper Smith, felt watching the sun rise was such an important gift to his life, he actually made mention of it in his will. He left his widow an estate of fifty-thousand dollars, and then he made this bequest to his other relatives:

"To my remaining relatives I give the sunshine, the birds and the bees, wherever the above mentioned sunshine, birds and bees may be found. The greatest art exhibit you will ever see opens daily at dawn. And equally wonderful, this exhibit is always free to those who view it."

How long has it been since you have awakened early to see the sun rise? This grand display of Gods creativity can ignite the creative gifts He placed in you and inspire you to use them during the day!

Working Together

As God's partners we beg you not to toss aside this
marvelous message of God's great kindness.
2 CORINTHIANS 6:1 TLB

Toyohiko Kagawa was a noted Japanese poet and Christian social reformer. Although he suffered poor health, he lived among the needy in the slums and worked tirelessly to overcome social injustice. His poem, "Work," speaks of die source of his strength:

WORK
I shall not say
That I am busy: —
Those who would help
The troubled people
Should expect to be
Busy always.
Christ was so thronged
By multitudes
He had no time to eat.
He said,

"To him that hath
Shall he given;
And from him that hath not
Shall be taken away
Even that
He seems to have."
Which means
That if we do not use
All of our powers
We lose them . . .
Then, too, the problem is
To do our work
With all our hearts;
We do not tire
Of doing what we love.
But most of all,
Our strength and comfort come
Only when God
Dwells in our souls
Working together with us.[7]

No matter what work you do today, you will work with purpose and strength if God is your partner. He is always with you, waiting for you to simply ask for His strength to finish the job!

Take Your Time

I delight in your decrees; I will not neglect your word.
PSALM 119:16

Frank was like many Christians. He had been taught that if he truly wanted God to guide his steps each day, he should spend time with God first thing every morning. He found a copy of a "Through the Bible in One Year" plan and got down to business: three chapters each morning and two each night.

Somehow though, the inspiration he expected to discover escaped him. He discussed the problem with his friend Carl. Frank said, "I wasn't sure how I would find the time to read the Bible every morning, but I manage to squeeze it in. Sometimes I have to rush through the chapters a little, but I always remember what I've read. You could quiz me on it and I'd get an 'A.' So why do I feel as if I haven't really read it?"

Carl answered, "It sounds to me as if you're reading the Bible the way you would a textbook. If you want to get into the meaning behind the words, pray before you read and ask God to reveal things to you. Instead of looking at the Bible as a reading assignment, think of it as a special meeting time with God—time you set aside to sit down and hear what He has to say to you."

"I get it," Frank said. "I was doing the old 'what's in it for me?' and expecting God to reward me for putting in the time."

"Give yourself more time to read and study," Carl suggested. "Even a few extra minutes can make a big difference. Just remember: the more time you give to God, the more time He gives back to you. Your day will go much better if you let *Him* set the pace and listen for what *He* has to say."

While it is important to read the Scriptures daily, it is far more important to read *until you sense in your spirit that God has said something to YOU*. Don't be concerned about reading a specific number of verses or chapters. The key is to read with a listening ear.

———————————————

The "To-Be List"

When the Holy Spirit controls our lives he will produce this kind of fruit in us: love, joy, peace, patience, kindness, goodness, faithfulness, gentleness and self-control.
GALATIANS 5:22-23 TLB

Nearly all of us face our day with a "to-do list." The Scriptures compel us, however, to have a "to-be list."

While it may be important to accomplish certain tasks, engage in certain projects, or have certain encounters during a day, what is more important *for eternity* is the person we *are* throughout the day.

From a "to-do" perspective, we tend to come before the Lord and say, "This is my list and this is my schedule. Please be with me, help me, and bless me."

From a "to-be" perspective, we might make these requests of the Lord:

- Help me to reflect Your love today.
- Help me to display Your joy.
- Help me to manifest Your peace.
- Help me to practice Your patience.
- Help me to express Your kindness.

- Help me to make known Your goodness.
- Help me to reveal Your faithfulness.
- Help me to show Your gentleness.
- Help me to exhibit Your self-control.

Wishful thinking does not produce these traits, however. They come from a life lived in communication with the Lord. They are the distinguishing marks of His presence in our lives. Our "to-be" list, therefore, must always begin with an invitation to the Holy Spirit to inspire us and impel us toward good works.

In order to *express* the Lord's kindness, for example, we first must see ourselves as *receiving* the Lord's kindness. In receiving His kindness, we become much more attuned to opportunities in which we might show His kindness to others. "Being kind" becomes a part of everything we do. The way we do our chores, hold our meetings, run our errands, and engage in our projects displays His kindness to those around us.

When we make our "to-be" list our top priority, the things we have "to do" become much more obvious—and far less burdensome!

No Darkness Here!

*But the path of the just is like the shining sun, that shines
ever brighter unto the perfect day.*
PROVERBS 4:18 NKJV

Once upon a time a Cave lived under the ground, as caves have the habit of doing. It had spent its lifetime in darkness.

One day it heard a voice calling to it, "Come up into the light; come and see the sunshine."

But the Cave retorted, "I don't know what you mean. There isn't anything but darkness." Finally the Cave was convinced to venture forth. He was amazed to see light everywhere and not a speck of darkness anywhere. He felt oddly warm and happy.

Turnabout was fair play and so, looking up to the Sun, the Cave said, "Come with me and see the darkness."

The Sun asked, "What is darkness?"

The Cave replied, "Come and see!"

One day the Sun accepted the invitation. As it entered the Cave it said, "Now show me your darkness." But there was no darkness!

The apostle John opens his Gospel account by describing Jesus as the Word and as the Light—"the true light that gives light to every man" (John 1:9 NIV). It is John who also records Jesus proclaiming, "I am the light of the world. Whoever follows me will never walk in darkness, but will have the light of life" (John 8:12 NIV).

Jesus made this statement at the close of a feast, just as giant candelabra were being extinguished throughout the city of Jerusalem. During the feast these lamps had illuminated the city so that night seemed to be turned to day. "My light is *not* extinguishable," Jesus was saying, "regardless of the times or seasons."

As this day begins, remember that you take the Light of the world with you; wherever you go and regardless of what may happen during your day, His light cannot be put out.

Everyday Benefits

Blessed be the Lord, who daily loads us with benefits.
PSALM 68:19 NKJV

Blessings we take for granted are often forgotten. Yet every day God "loads us with benefits." This morning think of some common things you may have taken for granted — and thank God for them:

• Lungs that work well and steadily — ten to fifteen times each minute.

• Bones that protect vital organs and muscles to hold the bones in their place.

• A healthy disease-fighting immune system.

• An untiring heart that pumps nine pints of blood through a 60,000-mile network of vessels.

• Body temperatures that remain constant.

• Our five senses — eyes to see the dawn, ears to hear your loved ones voice, a nose to smell the freshness of the early dew, the sense of touch to enjoy a hug, and the sense of taste to savor breakfast.

• Nerve cells that synapse and send messages to other parts of the body.

• A digestive system that brings nourishment to all the cells of the body.

• The ability—and desire—to get up and out of bed in the morning.

• A place to live and a place to work.

• Loving and supportive family, friends, and colleagues and the opportunities to let them know you care about them.

• An intimate relationship with God through Jesus Christ.

• The changing seasons that remind us of the different times of our lives.

• Each day's unique beauty—the angle of the sun, white clouds stretched out across the blue afternoon sky, the gold and pink sunset.

• The rotation of the earth that gives us day and night.

• Times for quiet reflection and grateful remembrances.

• The gift of laughter—and the ability to laugh at our mistakes.

Add your own blessings to this list and keep it growing all day long![8]

Out of the Dumps

Hope deferred makes the heart sick, but a longing fulfilled is
a tree of life.
P R O V E R B S   1 3 : 1 2

We all understand, perhaps too well, the meaning of the words "winter doldrums." We make it through December just line, no matter what the weather may be, because we are excitedly preparing for the Christmas and New Years holidays.

But then come January and February with snow, ice, subzero temperatures, and the post-holiday blues. Cabin fever sets in, the Christmas bills Hood the mailbox, tempers tend to fray, and each day seems like a carbon copy of the day before. In those areas of the world where the sun shines warmly all year, the winter doldrums may take on a little different twist — too many tourists causing crowded stores, crowded streets, and crowded restaurants.

Janet Leighton was suffering from this seasonal malady when, one day, she decided to break out of her doldrums. Bundling up against the cold, she took a walk in search of signs of hope . . . and she found them.

Red berries, purple briars, and golden grasses would seem insignificant in the spring, but in February they are the promise of more brilliant colors to come. They were enough of an encouragement to send Janet to her Bible, where she sought out well-loved verses and renewed her commitment to God.

The message of renewal seemed to snowball. She realized a friend for whom she had been praying was being healed gradually but surely. While paying bills, she saw other ways the Lord had blessed her family and her spirit was lifted.

Before the doldrums get you down, regardless of the season, take time to look for the splashes of color and signs of renewal God continually sends into your life. They're there . . . you just have to look for them![9]

Love and Faithfulness

Proclaim your love in the morning and your faithfulness at night.
P S A L M   9 2 : 2

The psalmist encourages us to proclaim the Lord's love in the morning.

This proclamation of love is not a matter of our echoing Elizabeth Barrett Browning in saying to the Lord, "How do I love thee? Let me count the ways . . ." Our love is not a recitation of the reasons why God is worthy of our love. Nor is it a declaration of our love for Him. Rather, our proclamation of love is to be a statement of how the Lord loves us!

How *does* He love us?

As you meditate on the Lords love for you, certain words come to mind. Certainly the Lord loves you unconditionally . . . gently . . . individually . . . intimately . . . eternally . . . closely . . . warmly . . .

tenderly . . . kindly. You are His child. He always has your good in mind. The apostle Paul said of Gods love:

"Who shall separate us from the love of Christ? For I am persuaded that neither death nor life, nor angels nor principalities nor powers, nor things present nor things to come, nor height nor depth, nor any other created thing, shall he able to separate us from the love of God which is in Christ Jesus our Lord."
ROMANS 8:35,38-39 NKJV

Proclaiming the Lords love for you in the morning will give you strength. Because you have a loving Father with you always, you can make it through any day, regardless of the surprises—good and bad—that come your way.

After beginning and walking through your day in Gods love, at the days end you can easily recount *His faithfulness.* He is faithful to provide what you need, deliver you from evil, and lead you into blessings—all of which are expressions of His love. In recognizing Gods love first and foremost, and living in that love all day long, you quickly recognize the *power* of God's love to sustain you, energize you, protect you—and give love to others.

This morning, accept and expect the Lord to be loving toward you . . . and by tonight, you will surely *know* He has been faithful!

No Room for Apathy

Sing praises to the Lord, which dwelleth in Zion: declare among the people his doings.
PSALM 9:11 KJV

Indifferent. Uninvolved. Middle of the road. Riding the fence. Uncommitted. Undecided. All of these words and phrases—none of which would be considered noble character traits—point toward one state of being: apathy.

While we might think apathy is a safe place in which to dwell, the Scriptures see it as a doomed existence. Jesus said to the church of Laodicea:

"I know thy works, that thou art neither cold nor hot: I would thou wert cold or hot. So then because thou art lukewarm, and neither cold nor hot, I will spew thee out of my mouth."
REVELATION 3:15-16 KJV

G.A. Studder-Kennedys poem describes the Lords sorrow over our apathy:

46

When Jesus came to Golgotha,
they hanged Him on a tree,
They drove great nails through hand and feet
and made a Calvary:
They crowned Him with a crown of thorns,
red were His wounds and deep,
For those were crude and cruel days,
and human flesh was cheap.
When Jesus came in modern day,
they simply passed Him by,
They never hurt a hair of Him,
they only let Him die:
For men had grown more tender,
and they would never give Him pain.
They only just passed down the street
and left Him in the rain.
Still Jesus cried, "Forgive them,
for they know not what they do:"
And still it rained the winter rain
that drenched Him through and through;
The crowd went home and left the streets
without a soul to see.
And Jesus crouched against a wall
and cried for Calvary.[10]

Choose to stand boldly for the Lord today!

———————————————

True Value

The last will be first, and the first will be last.
MATTHEW 20:16

I n the J.M. Barrie play, *The Admirable Crichton*, the Earl of Loam, his family, and several friends are shipwrecked on a desert island. These nobles were adept at chattering senselessly, playing bridge, and scorning poorer people. However, they could not build an outdoor fire, clean fish, or cook food — the very skills they needed to survive.

Stranded on a desert island, what the Earl's family and friends did know was entirely useless for their survival. Had it not been for their resourceful butler Crichton, they would have starved to death. He was the only one who possessed the basic skills to sustain life.

In a great turnabout, Crichton became the groups chief executive officer. He taught the Earl and his family and friends the skills they needed and organized their efforts to ensure their survival until their rescue.

It is always good to remind ourselves of our "relative" place in society. II we are on top, we need to remember we can soon be at the bottom. II we perceive ourselves as at the bottom, we need to know that in God's order we are among "the first."

In *The Finishing Touch,* Chuck Swindoll raises the issue of perceived significance by asking about the people behind these Christian greats:

Who taught Martin Luther his theology and inspired his translation of the New Testament?

Who visited with Dwight L. Moody at a shoe store and spoke to him about Christ?

Who was the elderly woman who prayed faithfully for Billy Graham for over twenty years?

Who found the Dead Sea Scrolls?

Who discipled George Mueller and snatched him from a sinful lifestyle?[11]

We may not achieve the fame and recognition from people that we would like to have in this life, but God doesn't call us to be well-known or admired. He calls us to be faithful to Him in whatever situation we find ourselves. When we are, we can see more clearly when he promotes us and gives us favor with others.

Run with Perseverance

Therefore, since we are surrounded by such a great cloud of witnesses, let us throw off everything that hinders and the sin that so easily entangles, and let us run with perseverance the race marked out for us.
HEBREWS 12:1

There may be no better feeling in the world than the joy of winning a race you were never expected to win!

Just ask Jenny Spangler. She won the women's marathon at the US Olympic Trials in February 1996, earning the right to compete at the Summer Olympic Games in Atlanta, Georgia.

At the time of the trials, Spangler was qualifier number 61, which meant that sixty runners had entered the race with faster limes than hers. No one had ever heard of her—and no one thought she could maintain a winning pace when she passed the leaders at the 16-mile mark.

Spangler had few successes to her credit. She had set an American junior record in the marathon during college, but then she left the sports scene after a stress fracture dashed her hopes in the Olympic Trials of 1984. Abandoning the sport after she ran poorly in 1988, she returned to school and earned a masters degree in business administration. She ran only two marathons between 1988 and 1996.

At the marathon trials, she was such an unknown that the second and third-place finishers asked each other, "Who is she?" after she took the lead and held on to it.

The favorites in February's race expected Spangler to lade, but she never did. Somewhere inside herself, she found the courage and stamina to finish strong. Not only did she make the Olympic team, but she took home first prize — $45,000.

Does the day ahead of you look as grueling as a marathon? Keep Jenny Spangler in mind as you jog through your various commitments and responsibilities. Believe you can get the job done. Run the race God has marked out before you. Keep moving!

You can end each day with the satisfaction of knowing you are that much closer to the goal!

Oh, Say, Can You See?

*We are hard pressed on every side, yet not crushed; we are
perplexed, but not in despair; persecuted, but not forsaken;
struck down, but not destroyed.*
2 CORINTHIANS 4:8-9 NKJV

Few of us think of the opening lines of our national
anthem, "The Star-Spangled Banner," as being
related to spiritual devotion—and yet they
certainly may be!

"Oh, say, can you see.
By the dawn's early light.
What so proudly we hailed
At the twilight's last gleaming . . ."

The composer of these lines, Francis Scott Key, had stood
on the ramparts of a ship and witnessed a fierce naval battle.
By the last rays of sunset, he had seen "Old Glory" waving
from a distant fort. Through the night, he had caught
glimpses of his nation's flag during flashes of light from
bursting cannons. But . . . would he see his flag, the symbol

of his freedom, flying at dawn? Or would he see another flag flying in its place, the battle lost?

He declares the answer in a later verse:

"The star-spangled banner
In triumph shall wave
O'er the land of the tree
And the home of the brave!"

Our level of faith at the close of a day may he very much like that of Francis Scott Key on that fateful night. We may have been in a battle against the enemy of our soul, have felt God's presence in our lives, but the attack has been so strong that we are tossing and turning during the night, wondering what the morning will bring.

When sunlight breaks through at dawn, the light of God's truth says: You are alive, God is still with you, and you will not be defeated!

While the war may not be over, yesterday's battle is finished. God is still on His throne. You are still His child. He has not abandoned you.

Face today with courage! Remember these lines as a member of the "nation" of Christ's own Body of believers, the Church:

"Praise the Power that hath made
and preserved us a nation!
Then conquer we must,
when our cause it is just.
And this be our motto,
'In God is our trust.'"

Awake My Soul!

But I will sing of your strength, in the morning I will sing of your love.
P S A L M   5 9 : 1 6

I t is not uncommon for a person to wake with the anticipated struggles of the day pressing on his or her mind. But life in Christ calls us to face the days challenges with the strength of the Holy Spirit stirring within.

Sometimes a sense of the Lord's presence needs to be rekindled, just as the still-glowing embers in a fireplace require stirring up in early morning hours to spark a new flame. The result is that both yesterdays embers and todays kindling come to a blaze.

What rekindles your spirit? Perhaps nothing brings the heart to life as quickly as songs of praise. Sing a new song to the Lord or your favorite praise and worship chorus. Giving voice to praise does more than awaken the senses—it awakens the soul to God's presence.

Even if you don't know the tune, reading these lyrics aloud is sure to stir your heart:

AWAKE MY SOUL

Awake, my soul, stretch every nerve.
And press with vigor on:
A heavenly race demands thy zeal.
And an immortal crown.
And an immortal crown.
A cloud of witnesses around
Holds thee in full survey:
Forget the steps already trod.
And onward urge tin wav.
And onward urge thy wav.
'Tis God's all animating voice
That calls thee from on high:
Tis His own hand presents the prize
To thine aspiring eve.
To thine aspiring eve.
Blest Saviour, introduced by Thee.
Have I mv race begun:
And, crowned with victory.
At Thy feet I'll lay mv honors down,
I'll lay mv honors down.[12]

True Identity

And because ye are sons, God hath sent forth the Spirit of his Son into your hearts, crying, Abba, Father.
GALATIANS 4:6 KJV

Every day the world challenges your identity by trying to tell you who you are—or ought to be—by shaping your desires, telling you what is important, what values you should have, and how to spend your time and resources. What the world is telling you may not be true!

The story is told of a rancher who had been hunting in the mountains of west Texas. Up high on a cliff he came across an eagles nest. He took one of the eagles eggs back to his ranch and placed it under one of his hens sitting on her eggs. Eventually the eagles egg hatched. The mother hen took care of the eaglet along with her baby chicks who hatched at the same time.

The eagle made its home in the barnyard along with the chickens. It ate, slept, and lived just like the chickens. One day an eagle from the nearby mountain swooped down over the barnyard in search of prey.

Trying to get her chicks and the eaglet to safety, the mother hen squawked loudly.

As the great eagle swooped low across the barnyard he also let out a harsh scream—a scream made only by eagles. The young chicks heeded their mothers warning, but the eaglet responded to the call of the eagle. He took flight and ascended, following the *eagle* to the mountain heights.

What does Scripture tell us about who we are as children of God? We are the apple of His eye (Zechariah 2:8); the flock of His people (Zechariah 9:16); a crown of glory in the hand of the Lord and a royal diadem in the hand of your God (Isaiah 62:3); the temple of God (1 Corinthians 3:17). We are heirs of God and joint heirs with Christ (Romans 8:17). We are kings and priests of our God (Revelation 5:10). We were created to bear His likeness (Genesis 1:27).

Most importantly, we are Gods children (1 John 3:1). We belong to Him and our hearts cry "Abba, Father!" when He calls to us.

Listen for His call today! Find out who you are and what your purpose is from Him, the One Who made you!

On the Road Again

For God did not give us a spirit of timidity, but a spirit of power, of love, and of self-discipline.
2 TIMOTHY 1:7

Getting yourself out of bed in the morning is one thing. Feeling prepared to face whatever comes your way that day is another. Where do you turn for a confidence-booster?

Believe it or not, one of the best confidence-builders you can find may be inside those fuzzy slippers you like to wear: your own two feet.

Researchers have discovered that regular exercise—thirty minutes, three or four times a week—boosts the confidence level of both men and women. This is due in part to the way exercise strengthens, tones, and improves the body's appearance. It also has to do with brain chemistry.

When a person exercises, changes take place inside the brain. Endorphins, released as one exercises, are proteins that work in the pleasure centers of the brain and make a person feel more exhilarated. When the heart rate increases during exercise, neurotrophins are also released, causing a person to feel more alert and focused.

Are you feeling anxious about your day? Take a walk, jog, cycle, or do some calisthenics first thing in the morning. See if you don't feel a little more on top of the world.

Those who exercise regularly also feel that if they can discipline themselves to exercise, they can discipline themselves to do just about anything!

The human body is one of the most awesome examples of Gods creative power — an example we live with daily. He has created us not only to draw confidence from reading His Word and experiencing His presence through prayer, but also from the use of our body.

Put on those walking shoes and talk with God as you go! Not only will your body become more fit and your mind more alert, but the Holy Spirit will give you direction and peace about your day.

———————————————

Personal Ideals

*He has shown you, O man, what is good; and what does the
Lord require of you but to do justly, to love mercy, and to
walk humble with your God?*
MICAH 6:8 NKJV

What do you hold to be your personal
ideals—the qualities you consider to be
foremost in defining good character?

This is what Sir William Osier once said about his
own ideals:

*"I have three personal ideals. One, to do the day's work
well and not to bother about tomorrow . . . The second ideal
has been to act the Golden Rule, as far as in me lay, toward
my professional brethren and toward the patients committed
to my care. And the third has been to cultivate such a
measure of equanimity as would enable me to bear success
with humility, the affection of my friends without pride, and
to be ready when the day of sorrow and grief come to meet it
with the courage befitting a man."*

A speech teacher once assigned her students to give
a one-sentence speech, entitled "What I Would Like for
My Tombstone to Read." The class told her later that

this assignment was one of the most challenging assignments they had ewer received. In virtually every case, the students saw a great discrepancy between the way they lived their lives and the way they desired their lives to be perceived by others.

Many of us make New Years resolutions to "turn over a new leaf." We greet a new day with a vow or determination to "do better" in a certain area of our lives. But rarely do we give diligent thought to what we consider the highest and noblest pursuits in life.

This morning, give some thought to what *you* hold to be the characteristics of a respected life. What do *you* aspire to in your own character?

As you identify these trails, you can then see more clearly how you desire to live your life and what must change in order to live up to your ideals.

———————————————

Where Does the Time Go?

While it is daytime, I must continue doing the work of the One who sent me. Night is coming, when no one can work.
JOHN 9:4 NCV

Most of us look around and find reminders of good intentions. We readily see areas where we never followed through to reach a goal. The seldom-used exercise equipment needs dusting. A piano, intended to fulfill our dreams of happy family sing-a-longs, sits silent.

The books piled on the nightstand remain to be read. And the laptop computer we intended to take on vacation to write a novel is still in its original packaging.

More importantly, there are the children in our family who wait for our attention. Every child has gifts and abilities waiting to be developed—but that takes time.

To tap into potential takes intentional, concerted effort. It doesn't just happen. Time for meaningful interaction and activity doesn't always "appear" to us as we juggle a full day of appointments and other commitments.

The time God gives to us is ours to spend—we determine how to use it. We can lill it with life-building activities, or we can let it silt through our lingers hour by hour, day by day, week by week, until before we know it, an entire year is gone and very little accomplished.

As long as you are alive, your time—24 hours, 1,440 minutes, 86.400 seconds a day—*will* be spent. It is up to you to decide *how* you are going to spend it.

Accept the challenge to make every moment count! When you take your child to the dentist, make it an adventure, a time to listen, learn, and share God's wisdom. Is there a free hour when you can sit quietly and read a chapter or two in one of those books?

Look at what you have planned for today and set your priorities according to the goals you have set for your life. Do the same thing tomorrow and the next day. It won't be long before your life will begin to be more productive and more fulfilling.

———————————

Hope for the Best

*Whatever happens, conduct yourselves in a manner worthy
of the gospel of Christ.*
PHILIPPIANS 1:27

W hat if I fail? What if I lose? What if he
hates me? What if she yells at me?

These are the types of questions that
often go through our minds when we are faced with
difficult decisions or trying circumstances. II we speak
up and say the wrong thing, how will we ever repair
the damage? If we act too hastily and then fail, how
can we ever look our loved ones in the eye?

An insurance company executive faced these fears
soon after assuming a supervisory post. She had
realized that many of her employees were being paid
less than employees in other departments who were
doing basically the same type of work.

As a new boss, she knew it was risky to challenge
upper management. What would they think of her?
However, for the sake of her employees she felt
compelled to overcome these fears and act on their
behalf. How could she do that?

She asked herself a more important question: "What is the worst that could happen if I . . . ?" Someone could get angry—but that would pass. Raises could be refused—but at least she would have tried. She could lose her job—but she was confident God would supply another.

Trusting God for a good outcome and refusing to give in to her fears, she decided to approach upper management about the discrepancies. When she did, they not only took her concern seriously, but began to do something about the problem.

In whatever situation you find yourself, God is with you to help you sort it out, look at it from different angles, and ultimately see it from His perspective. Then you can act according to His will and trust Him completely for a great outcome.

Today, live your life God's way! Not only will you see tremendous growth and victory, but He will surround your life with favor.

More than Positive Thinking

For as he thinks in his heart, so is he.
PROVERBS 23:7 NKJV

Wat we think about determines what we do. Even more important, the Scriptures tell us what we think about shapes our attitudes and how we live our lives.

The Greek city of Philippi was one of the places where the apostle Paul had a fruitful ministry. The Greeks were great thinkers. They loved a good debate, a lively conversation about philosophy, or a rousing time of oratory that might trigger the imagination. Paul wrote to the Philippians:

"Whatever things are true, whatever things are noble, whatever things are just, whatever things are pure, whatever things are lovely, whatever things are of good report, if there is any virtue and if there is anything praiseworthy –
meditate on these things."
PHILIPPIANS 4:8 NKJV

It's interesting to note Paul wrote this immediately after addressing three other concerns in Philippians, chapter 4. First, he tells two women who are having an argument to become of "the same mind in the Lord." Paul wants them to be at peace with each other and to rejoice together in the Lord.

Second, Paul tells them to be gentle with all men. That's descriptive of having peace with those who don't know the Lord. And third, Paul advises them not to be anxious or worried about anything, but to turn all their troubles over to the Lord. He wants them to have total peace of mind and heart.

Paul is encouraging the Philippians to become God's "peace people" by turning their thoughts toward God's blessings and Word. He makes it very clear what the result will be:

> " . . . and the God of peace will be with you."
> PHILIPPIANS 4:9

As we look for the good in others, and meditate on the unending goodness of our Creator, we find the path toward peace with others and the peace that passes all understanding in whatever situation we find ourselves.

Thinking right is more than positive thinking, it is living a life that is filled with God's goodness, wisdom, and mercy!

A Leap of Faith

The righteous shall he glad in the Lord, and shall trust in him; and all the upright in heart shall glory.
P S A L M   6 4 : 1 0   K J V

I n his book about cameraman Neil Davis, *One Crowded Hour*, Tim Bowden tells about an incident that happened in Borneo in 1964 during the military confrontation between Malaysia and Indonesia.

A group of Nepalese Gurkhas were asked if they would jump from transport planes into combat against the Indonesians if the need arose. The Gurkhas had never been trained as paratroopers and were assured of their right to turn down the request. Bowden quotes Davis' account:

"Now the Gurkhas usually agreed to anything, but on this occasion they provisionally rejected the plan. But the next day one of the NCOs sought out the British officer who made the request and said they had discussed the matter further and would be prepared to lump under certain conditions.

'What are they?' asked the British officer.

The Gurkhas told him they would jump if the land was marshy or reasonably soft without rocky outcrops, because they were inexperienced at falling. The British officer considered this, and said that the dropping area would almost certainly he over jungle, and there would not be rocky outcrops, so that seemed all right. Was there anything else?

'Yes,' said the Gurkhas. They wanted the plane to fly as slowly as possible and no more than one hundred feet high. The British officer pointed out the planes always did fly as slowly as possible when dropping troops, but to jump from one hundred feet was impossible, because the parachutes would not open in time from that height.

'Oh,' said the Gurkhas, 'that's all right, then. We'll jump with parachutes anywhere. You didn't mention parachutes before!'"[13]

Remember today that God is your pilot and parachute! It's always safe to jump on His command.

Facing the Impossible

Without faith it is impossible to please Him.
HEBREWS 11:6 NKJV

How often have you heard the words, "It can't be done"? Perhaps you were the one who said those words. We should not take up every impossible challenge just to prove we can do it. However, there are worthwhile things that need to he done which look impossible or haven't yet been done.

Has God given you a vision or dream? Often the one who has the inspiration also must have the "perspiration"—the energy and motivation to do it. If you are facing a formidable challenge today, this poem by Edgar Guest is for you.

IT COULDN'T BE DONE
Somebody said that it couldn't be done,
But he with a chuckle replied
That "maybe it couldn't," be he would be one

Who wouldn't say so till he'd tried.
So he buckled right in with the trace of a grin
On his face, If he worried he hid it.
He started to sing as he tackled the thing
That wouldn't be done, and he did it.

Somebody scoffed: "Oh, you'll never do that:
At least no one ever has done it";
But he took off his coat and he took off his hat,
And the first thing we knew he'd begun it.
With a lift of his chin and a bit of a grin.
Without any doubting or quiddit,
He started to sing as he tackled the thing
That couldn't be done, and he did it.

There are thousands to tell you it cannot be done;
There are thousands to prophesy failure;
There are thousands to point out to you, one by one,
The dangers that wait to assail you.
But just buckle in with a bit of a grin,
Just take off your coat and go to it;
Just start to sing as you tackle the thing
That "cannot be done." and you'll do it.[14]

When we know what God has called us to do, we can also know He has provided the wherewithal to get the job done!

―――――――――――――――――――――

See the Light

For thou art my lamp, O Lord; and the Lord illumines my darkness.
2 SAMUEL 22:29 NASB

Helen Keller may have lost her ability to see, hear, and speak at a very early age, but she did not lose her gift of inspiring others.

In her many books and through a world tour designed to promote the education of others who shared her disabilities, Keller spoke eloquently on the subject of darkness—the kind that invades the hearts and minds of the sighted:

"Truly I have looked into the very heart of darkness, and refused to yield to its paralyzing influence, but in spirit I am one of those who walk the morning. What if all dark, discouraging moods of the human mind come across my way as thick as the dry leaves of autumn? Other feet have traveled that road before me, and I know the desert leads to God as surely as the given, refreshing fields and fruitful orchards. I too have been profoundly humiliated, and brought to realize my littleness amid the immensity of

72

creation. The more I learn, the less I think I know, and the more I understand of my sense-experience, the more I perceive its shortcomings and its inadequacy as a basis of life. Sometimes the points of view of the optimist and the pessimist are placed before me so skillfully balanced that only by sheer force of spirit can I keep my hold upon a practical, livable philosophy of life. But I use my will, choose life and reject its opposite – nothingness."[15]

When the day ahead of you seems shadowed or darkness threatens to overcome you, choose life! Take Helen Keller's words to heart and reject "nothingness" by turning to the Lord. He will bring light into your soul and joy into your heart.

The Bulldog Way

And let us not be weary in well doing; for in due season we shall reap, if we faint not.
GALATIANS 6:9 KJV

Are you in the midst of a frustrating struggle? Before you throw in the towel, remember this story about the bulldog.

A man once owned two very fine bird dogs, and he had spent many hours training them. One day he looked out his window just in time to see an ugly little bulldog digging his way under the fence into his bird dogs' yard. As the dog wriggled under the fence, the man realized it was too late to stop him.

He thought to himself how uneven the fight would be. The poor little bulldog was surely no match for his animals. Snipping, barking, growling—tails and ears flying—the battle raged. When the little dog had had enough, he trotted back to the hole under the fence and shimmied out.

Amazed that none of the dogs looked any the worse for the light, he didn't give the incident another thought until the next day, when he saw the little

74

bulldog coming down the sidewalk toward the hole in the fence. To his amazement, a repeat performance of the previous days battle began. And once again, the little bulldog picked his moment to end the light, left the bird dogs barking and snarling, and casually slid back under the fence.

Day after day for over a week the unwelcome visitor returned to harass his bigger canine counterparts. Then the man was obliged to leave for a week on business. When he returned, he asked his wife about the on-going battle.

"Battle?" she replied, "Why there hasn't been a battle in four days."

"He finally gave up?" asked the bird dog owner.

"Not exactly," she said. "That ugly little dog still comes around every day . . . he even shimmied under the fence until a day or so ago. But now all he has to do is *walk* past the hole and those bird dogs tuck their tails and head for their doghouse whining all the way."

Sometimes persistence is the key to success!

———————————————————

Never Give Up

Forgetting what is behind and straining toward what is ahead, I press on toward the goal to win the prize for which God has called me heavenward in Christ Jesus.
PHILIPPIANS 3:13-14

Fire is a gift—of warmth, light, beauty, and utility. Nothing beats a crackling fire on a cold winter's night, and who hasn't enjoyed roasting marshmallows over an open fire? But fire also can be an enemy. Sometimes it destroys the things we love.

On January 29, 1996, a blaze consumed one of Venice's most treasured buildings: the 204-year-old opera house, La Fenice. Hundreds of Venetians stood and watched as the building went up in flames.

Cause for sadness? Definitely. Cause for despair? Absolutely not. The construction of La Fenice had been delayed by fire in 1792. Another fire in 1836 had forced the Venetians to rebuild. And so too, after the fire in 1996 Venetians are already rallying to rebuild their opera house.

Interestingly, La Fenice means "the phoenix," referring to the mythological Egyptian bird that died in a fiery nest, only to emerge from the ashes as a brand-new bird. It is in that spirit the Venetians rebuild.

Can we restore what the fires in our lives destroy? Sometimes. If we desire to rebuild and we truly believe it is what the Lord would have us do, we put our full effort into the task. At other times when the Lord brings us through a fire, His desire is for the old to be left in ashes so something entirely *different* can be constructed on the site. This is true not only in the physical world in which we live, but also in the interior world of our souls, when our inner mettle is "tried by fire."

In those cases when we can't or shouldn't rebuild, we can remember Shadrach, Meshach, and Abed-nego. They were thrown into Nebuchadnezzar's fiery furnace for refusing to bow to an idol. (See Daniel, chapter 3.) Like them, we can emerge stronger and better after having been tested. We can see our lives touch and inspire others by standing up for what we believe.

If you are facing calamity or disaster today, the Bible tells you to quickly put it behind you by rebuilding or building something new. Whichever God desires, you will become stronger and better than before if you "press on!"

The Morning News

*For thus says the Lord: Sing aloud with gladness for Jacob,
and shout at the head of the nations. Proclaim, praise, and
say, The Lord has saved His people.*
JEREMIAH 31:7 AMP

Whether on the radio by the bed, the TV set next to the breakfast table, or the car stereo, the morning news is part of the vast majority of households in our nation. While we decry the negative message of most news items, we seem addicted to hearing more and more news. The result: we allow more and more negativism into our national psyche. If we add feature programs that claim to be "informative" about human nature—including sensational talk-show programs—we only increase the negative influence on our lives.

The Gospel shines in sharp contrast.

The word "gospel" is derived from an early Anglo-Saxon word "godspel." It meant "good tidings" and later took on the meaning "God-story," or the story of God's love shown to us through the sacrifice of His Son, Jesus Christ. The Gospel is *good news*.

How do we shine the light of the Gospel on the darkness of the worlds news reports? One way is to proclaim the goodness of Jesus Christ every time we hear a negative report.

Is the report about crime? Then we proclaim, "Jesus can change the hearts of the most hardened criminals. He can heal the wounds of those who are victimized. Even so, have mercy, Lord Jesus."

Is the story about racial tension, war, or a conflict among ethnic groups? Then we proclaim, "Come, Lord Jesus. Be the Prince of Peace in this situation."

Is the news story about sickness, disease, or epidemic? Then we proclaim, "Jesus is the Healer. Make us whole. Lord Jesus."

Is the story about a natural catastrophe, storm, or accident? We proclaim, "Jesus calms the storms and brings about good from evil. Come and reign. Lord Jesus. Renew us with Your life."

Even if we stop watching negative television programming and try to avoid anything ungodly, we will still hear negative news and encounter difficult circumstances. However, when we hear a bad report, we can counteract it with a good word about the Lord Jesus Christ, our Good News. He is the best news report any person can ever hear.

Grace for Today

*For all have sinned and fall short of the glory of God, and are
justified freely by his grace.*
ROMANS 3:23-24

I n *The Grace of Giving*, Stephen Olford gives an
account of Peter Miller, a Baptist pastor who
lived during the American Revolution. He lived
in Ephrata, Pennsylvania, and enjoyed the friendship
of George Washington.

Michael Wittman also lived in Ephrata. He was an
evil-minded man who did all he could to oppose and
humiliate the pastor.

One day Michael Wittman was arrested for treason
and sentenced to die. Peter Miller traveled the seventy
miles to Philadelphia on foot to plead for the life of the
traitor.

"No, Peter," General Washington said, "I cannot
grant you the life of your friend."

"My friend!" exclaimed the old preacher. "He's the
bitterest enemy I have."

"What?" exclaimed Washington, "You've walked
seventy miles to save the life of an enemy? That puts

the matter in a different light. I'll grant your pardon." And he did.

Peter Miller took Michael Witt man back home to Ephrata — no longer an enemy but a friend.

Millers example id grace and forgiveness flowed from his knowledge of Gods sacrifice for the human race. Because God forgave him and sacrificed His Son for him, he found the grace to sacrifice for his enemy. Although most of us know Gods grace and love for us is great, sometimes we have to be reminded that His love never fails — even when we do!

At the Pan American Games, a United States diver was asked how he coped with the stress of international diving competition. He replied that he climbed to the board, took a deep breath, and thought, "Even if I blow this dive, my mother will still love me." Then he would strive for excellence.

At the beginning of each day, take a deep breath and say, "Even if I blow it today, my God will still love me." Then, assured of His grace and quickness to forgive, go into the day seeking a perfect score!

Making Connections

My help comes from the Lord who made heaven and earth.
P S A L M   1 2 1 : 1 2   N K J V

I n *Silent Strength for My Life,* Lloyd John Ogilvie tells the story of a young hoy he met while traveling. He noticed the boy waiting alone in the airport lounge for his flight to he called. Boarding began for the flight, and the young child was sent ahead of the adult passengers to find his seat. When Ogilvie got on the aircraft, he discovered the hoy had been assigned the scat next to his.

The boy was polite when Ogilvie engaged him in conversation and then quietly spent time coloring in an airline coloring book. He showed neither anxiety nor worry about the flight as preparation was made for takeoff.

During the flight, the plane flew into a very bad storm, which caused the jetliner to bounce around like a "kite in the wind." The air turbulence and subsequent pitching and lurching of the aircraft frightened some of the passengers, but the young boy seemed to take it all in stride.

A female passenger seated across the aisle from the boy became alarmed by the wild rolling of the aircraft. She asked the boy, "Little boy, aren't you scared?"

"No, Ma'am," he replied, looking up just briefly from his coloring book. "My dad's the pilot."

There are times when events in our lives make us feel like we are in the middle of a turbulent storm. Try as we might, we cannot seem to land on solid ground or get a sure footing. We may have the sensation of being suspended in mid-air with nothing to hold on to, nothing to stand on, and no sure way to get to safety.

In the midst of the storm, however, we can remember that our Heavenly Father is our pilot. Despite the circumstances, our life is in the hands of the One who created heaven and earth.

If uncontrollable fear begins to rise within you today, say to yourself. "My Dad's the pilot!"[16]

The People Factor

Greater love hath no man than this, that a man lay down his life for his friends.
JOHN 15:13 KJV

———————————————

Wanted: Someone willing to risk his life to rescue 200 Jewish artists and intellectuals from the Nazis. Faint of heart need not apply.

Would you jump at the chance to take on this job? Varian Fry did. A high-school Latin teacher from Connecticut, he went to Marseilles, France, in August 1941, intending to stay only three weeks. He stayed fourteen months.

Forging passports and smuggling people over the mountains into Spain, Fry and a handful of American and French volunteers managed to save almost 4,000 people from the Nazi scourge. Among them were the 200 well-recognized Jewish artists and intellectuals he originally intended to rescue.

Did Fry have a difficult time motivating himself each day to face the task in front of him? Probably not.

He had little doubt what he was doing had divine purpose and tremendous significance.

Most of us will never find ourselves in Fry's position, and often we wonder if what we do throughout our day has any significance at all. In many cases, it takes more strength to do the trivial tasks than the monumental ones.

If the job we do is difficult, we must ask God to show us how to make the task less strenuous.

If the job is dull, we need to ask God to reveal ways to make it more interesting.

If we think our work is unimportant, we need to remember that being in God's will and doing a good job for Him will not only bring blessing to others, but blessing to us now and for eternity.

Often it is the *people* factor that keeps us motivated. God gives us purpose and makes our lives meaningful, but He is always working to bless us so we can turn around and bless other people.

The tasks you face today are significant as you work to meet a need or to see growth in others. You will see God's love moving through your life to others in everything you do for them—from putting a bandage on a child's skinned knee to inventing a machine which helps people with asthma breathe.

Enjoying the Scenery

The earth is full of the goodness of the Lord.
PSALM 33:5 NKJV

Every day has moments worth savoring and enjoying to the fullest. It may take some effort to search out those moments, but the reward is a sense of enriched meaning in life, which is in turn, motivating and satisfying.

Watch your children scamper for the school bus . . . or play freely in a warm spring rain shower . . . or enjoy observing the movement of a caterpillar on a leaf.

Take your brown-bag lunch to the park and watch the geese circle on the pond or elderly men bowl on the green.

Gaze out a window and watch birds making their nest on a ledge, or the careful balancing act of window washers at work on the building across the boulevard.

Enjoy a steaming cup of cappuccino in a garden-room cafe while a string ensemble plays in the background.

Watch puppies tumble about in their play or a kitten play with a ball of yarn.

Linger at a balcony rail with a glass of tangy lemonade watching the sun set in golden glory.

Harol V. Melchert once said:

"Live your life each day as you would climb a mountain. An occasional glance toward the summit keeps the goal in mind, but main beautiful scenes are to be observed from each new vantage point. Climb slowly, steadily, enjoying each passing moment; and the view from the summit will serve as a fitting climax for the journey."

Gods creation is all around us — not only in the form of foliage, animals, and birds, but in people. Take time today to enjoy what God has done and is doing! You'll enjoy what you are doing more.

———————————————

Winning Preparation

The horse is made ready for the day of battle, but victory rests with the Lord.
PROVERBS 21:31

Lexington, Kentucky is renowned for producing the finest thoroughbred race horses in the world. More than 140 horse farms are located within the city limits and on the outskirts of the city. But it's not just the beautiful acreage that draws serious breeders to buy farms or horses in that area. The Kentucky Bluegrass area has something that cannot be found in such abundance anywhere else on earth—a particular type of limestone that lies just the right distance under the surface of the ground, continuously releasing vital minerals into the soil.

Plants grown in this soil, such as the grass the horses cat, are rich in the precise combination of minerals needed to build extremely strong but very light bones—ideal for racing. Thus, a colt eating Kentucky bluegrass spends his first two years eating exactly what will help him win the race of his life!

Along the same line, consider the habits of the Alaskan bull moose. The older males of the species battle for dominance during the fall breeding season, literally going head-to-head with their giant racks of antlers. Often the antlers, their only weapons, are broken. When this happens, the moose with the broken antlers will assuredly be defeated.

The heftiest moose with the largest and strongest antlers almost always triumphs. Therefore, the battle fought in the fall is really won in the summer when the>r do nothing but eat. The one that consumes the best diet for growing antlers and gaining weight will be the heavyweight in the fall. Those that eat inadequately have weaker antlers and less bulk.

There is a spiritual lesson here for all of us. Battles await us, and we must Ire prepared. Enduring faith, strength, and wisdom for trials can be developed before they are needed by spending time with God.

Choose today to steep yourself in God's Word and to spend time with Him in prayer. If troubles arise later, you will be attuned to your Fathers voice and be able to get His battle plan—which is always the winning one!

Lord of the Dance

You have turned for me my mourning into dancing.
PSALM 30:11 NKJV

Scripture records times of rejoicing that were celebrated with dancing. The children of Israel danced after crossing the Red Sea and in celebration of military victory. King David danced before the Lord when the Ark of the Covenant was brought to the City of David. When the prodigal son returned, his lather prepared a feast that included music and dancing.

Each day we are invited to dance and celebrate all life has for us. In this Sydney Carter hymn, Jesus is "Lord of the Dance."

I danced in the morning when the world was begun,
And I danced in the moon and the stars and the sun,
And I came down from heaven and I danced on the earth.
At Bethlehem I had my birth.
I danced for the scribe and the Pharisee,
But they would not dance and they would not follow me;
I danced lor the fishermen, lor James and John;

They came to me and the dance went on.
I danced on the Sabbath when I cured the lame,
The holy people said it was a shame;
They whipped and they stripped and they hung me high;
And they left me there on a cross to die.
I danced on a Friday and the sky turned black;
It's hard to dance with the devil on your back;
They buried my body and they thought I'd gone,
But I am the dance and I still go on.
They cut me down and I leapt up high,
I am the life that'll never, never die;
I'll live in you iI you'll live in me;
I am the Lord of the Dance, said he.
Dance, then, wherever you may be;
I am the Lord of the Dance, said he.
And I'll lead you all wherever you may be,
and I'll lead you all in the dance, said he.[17]

Dancing is one way we can celebrate God in worship and joy. When we start each day with Jesus we are His partner in the dance of life.

Taking a Stand

Be strong and of a good courage, fear not, nor be afraid of them: for the Lord thy God, he it is that doth go with thee; he will not fail thee, nor forsake thee.
DEUTERONOMY 31:6

Nine-year-old Kevin was upset at learning one of his favorite Popsicle flavors was being discontinued. But what's a kid going to do? Fighting City Hall when you're under voting age can seem like a fruitless endeavor.

"But you're a consumer," the boy's mother said. "Yes,Yes, you can make a difference. You can start a protest. You can stand up and be counted." So Kevin took his mothers advice.

With the help of his cousins, Kevin launched a petition drive, eventually gathering 130 signatures. The children also constructed picket signs with catchy sayings. Finally, on a rainy January day, Kevin and nearly a dozen family members marched at the Popsicle's headquarters.

The company's CEO saw the marchers from the window of his office and invited them inside. He listened to the children's pleas and then explained the company's position. Extensive marketing research had been done, and thousands of dollars had already been spent to present a new flavor. In the end, however, Kevin and his group won the day. The CEO decided to forget the new flavor and grant the petitioners' plea to return the old flavor to the marketplace.

Never give in to the notion that you are too insignificant to lead the move toward a positive change in your world. As a band leader once pointed out in an inspirational speech to a group of students: the smallest person in the band, the head twirler, is the one who is leading us down the street!

The Lord expects each of us to be bold enough to speak His truth whenever the opportunity arises. Sometimes truth is best expressed in conversations, letters, or face-to-face encounters. Sometimes truth may need to be expressed with placards and petitions. In either case, *one person* begins the process by deciding to take a stand. You can be that person today.

———————————————

The Giving Factor

Give, and it will be given to you; good measure, pressed down, shaken together, running over.
LUKE 6:38 NASB

Much of our day is spent in getting. We *get* up in the morning in order to *get* a good breakfast before we *get* a ride to work. We *get* in gear and *get* the job done so we can *get* a paycheck that will pay for a getaway on the weekend so we might *get* rest to get a jump on the coming week!

The Gospel challenges us to become people who are more concerned about giving than getting. Giving sounds noble, and we instinctively know it's the "right thing to do," but in practice, giving is difficult. Genuine giving involves concern for others, and ultimately it requires the demolition of pride and self-centeredness. Giving is a sacrifice, letting go of at least part of that which we believe to be "ours."

The great mystery is that in giving, we get. What we get may not be what we had originally intended to get. Yet those who are generous in their giving repeatedly say: what they get in return is always far more valuable and meaningful than what they gave or what they had originally intended to get.

Norman Vincent Peale once said:

"The man who lives for himself is a failure. Even if he gains much wealth, position, or power, he is still a failure. The man who lives for others has achieved true success. A rich man who consecrates his wealth and his position to the good of humanity is a success. A poor man who gives of his service and his sympathy to others has achieved true success, even though material prosperity or outward honors never come to him."

Find a way to give *something* to someone in need today, whether of your money, time, talent, effort, service, tears, laughter, ideas, or possessions. Give freely and generously, not motivated by a payback. The payback will come, but let its arrival be a joyful surprise in your day!

Gravitational Pull

Let as also lay aside every weight and the sin that clings so closely, and let us run with perseverance the race that is set before us.
HEBREWS 12:1 NRSV

In 1969, millions of people watched the televised Apollo 11 takeoff that launched three men into space. Those three men would become the first humans to land on the moon. Many people remember exactly where they were when they saw astronaut Neil Armstrong take those historic first steps on the moon. We were eyewitnesses to one of the greatest achievements in history!

One of the remarkable facts about this space trip was that more energy was used in the first few minutes during and after liftoff than during the next several days of traveling half a million miles to the moon. Tremendous energy was needed to break out of the earth's powerful gravitational pull.

Likewise, inertia is hard to overcome in life. We may feel it takes more energy to get us "launched" in the morning than it does to get us through the day!

Bad habits, past hurts, bitterness, half-hearted commitment, and unconfessed sin can all be weights that slow us down or keep us from going upward and onward with the Lord.

"The secret of daily life is this," says Macrina Wiederkehr, a Benedictine nun. "There are no leftovers! There is nothing—no thing, no person, no experience, no thought, no joy or pain—that cannot be harvested and used for nourishment on our journey to God."

We may think losing a job or a business failure will prevent us from ever going forward in our career. We may be convinced a difficult childhood will keep us from healthy, loving relationships. Or we may feel that a physical limitation will keep us from true fulfillment. Not so in Gods kingdom!

Nothing that happens to us is wasted by the Lord. He uses everything for His life-building purposes when we give all our experiences to Him.

This morning, give each weight or encumbrance that drags you down to God. Then watch them become fuel to propel you out of the "gravitational pull" of bad experiences and into the joy of the Lord!

———————————————

Deep Roots

*So then, just as you received Christ Jesus as Lord, continue
to live in him, rooted and built up in him, strengthened in
the faith as you were taught, and overflowing with
thankfulness.*
COLOSSIANS 2:6-7

A writer for a local newspaper was interviewing a farmer about the effects of recent weather on his crops. Rain had been abundant and the farmers soybean and corn crops were tall and lush.

"My crops are especially vulnerable right now," said the farmer. This statement took the reporter by surprise. He had planned to focus his article on the good harvest expected and the economic boom it would bring for the town.

The farmer went on, "Even a short drought could have a devastating effect."

"Why?" asked the reporter.

The farmer explained that while we see frequent rains as a benefit, during rainy times the plants are not required to push their roots deep in search of water.

The roots remain near the surface, leaving the plants unprepared for drought.

His crop also faced the danger of sudden strong wind storms. Again, because of the shallow root structure, a strong wind could wipe him out in only a few minutes.

Some Christians enjoy an abundance of "rain showers" that come in the form of praise services, fellowship with other believers, and times of rich Bible teaching. But when stress enters their lives, these same Christians can lose faith, abandon God, or believe God to be unfaithful. Why? Their roots have never pushed much below the surface.

Their spiritual life is top-heavy, relying on others more than on personal devotion in prayer and study of Gods Word. They are especially vulnerable to the strong winds of adversity or the searing heat of stress.

Only the roots grown deep into God will help us endure tough times. Put your roots down more deeply today. Spend time with the Lord . . . in the Word . . . and on your knees.

Shake it Up

Therefore, gird your minds for action.
1 PETER 1:13 NASB

Sometimes our daily routine seems more like a never-ending rut. The activities and responsibilities that were once fresh and new gradually become stale and old. What can you do to shake things up a bit?

A woman asked herself that question one morning as she arose at her usual time. She had done all she needed to do to get her children off to school and her husband to work. Now she was home alone, looking for the motivation to face her day.

She said to herself, *I know what I'll do. I'll turn things upside-down. Instead of sticking to my usual schedule, I'll reverse the order.*

That meant her first item of business was preparing dinner. She thought she might feel strange preparing meat and vegetables at 9am, but she was surprised to find she fell a sense of relief at having this "chore" done early. Somehow, it made the rest of the housework and errands less stressful.

She found a little extra time to write a letter and catch up on some reading, and by the time her children came tromping in from school, she felt happier than she had in weeks. She was already thinking of other ways to add variety to her daily routine.

Who says you have to do the same things in the same way at the same time every day?

The Bible clearly tells us that our God is a God of infinite variety! While His commandments are not negotiable. His methods often change. That's part of His nature as our Creator. The Lord is continually creating new methods to reach us with His love and to show us His care.

Break out of your rut today! Ask the Lord to give you insight into how you might participate more fully in His creative process by doing things differently.

———————————————————————

Jigsaw Puzzle

Looking away [from all that will distract] to Jesus, who is the leader and the source of our faith [giving the first incentive for our belief] and is also its finisher [bringing it to maturity and perfection].
HEBREWS 12:2 AMP

Are you a jigsaw puzzle aficionado?

If you have ever worked a complicated jigsaw puzzle, you know three things about them:

First, they take time. Few people can put several hundred pieces of a puzzle together rapidly. Most large and complex puzzles take several days, even weeks, to complete. The fun is in the *process*, the satisfaction in the *accomplishment*.

Second, the starting point of a puzzle is usually to identify the corners and edges, the pieces with a straight edge.

Third, jigsaw puzzles are fun to work by oneself, but even more fun to work with others. When a "fit" is discovered between two or more pieces, the excitement is felt by all the participants.

Consider the day ahead of you like a piece in the jigsaw puzzle of your life. Indeed, its shape is likely to be just as jagged, its colors just as unidentifiable. The meaning of today may *not* be sequential to that of yesterday. What you experience today may actually *fit* with something you experienced several months ago, or something you will experience in the future. You aren't likely to see the big picture of your life by observing only one day. Even so, you can trust that there is a plan and purpose. All the pieces will come together according to Gods design and timetable.

On some days, we find straight-edged pieces of our life's puzzle — truths that become a part of our reason for being. On other days, we find pieces that fit together so we understand more about ourselves and about God's work in our lives. And on all days, we can know the joy of sharing our lives with others and inviting them to be part of the process of discovering who we are.

The main thing to remember is to enjoy the process. Live today to the fullest, knowing one day you'll see the full picture.

Active Faith

Let us not give up meeting together, as some are in the habit
of doing, but let us encourage one another.
H E B R E W S   1 0 : 2 5

Philip Haille went to the little village of Le Chambon, France, to write about a people who, unlike other villages, had hidden their Jews from the Nazis. Fie wondered what caused them to risk their lives to do such extraordinary good.

He interviewed people in the village and was overwhelmed — not by their extraordinary qualities, but by their *ordinariness*. They were not an unusually bright, quick-witted, brave, or discerning people.

Haille looked for possible connections between the citizens' lives to find the reason they had done what no other French town had done. In the end, the author concluded that the one factor uniting them to do good was their attendance at their little church.

Sunday after Sunday they heard the sermons of Pastor Trochme. Over time they became people who knew what was right and obtained the courage from God to do it. When it came time for them to act boldly

—as on the day the Nazis came to town—they quietly did what was right.

One elderly woman faked a heart attack when the Nazis came to search her house. She told Haille about her personal dramatic ploy "Pastor always taught us that there comes a time in every life when a person is asked to do something for Jesus. When my time came, I just *knew* what to do."

There were two strong beliefs that gave the citizens of this town inner strength of steel. First, they knew their spiritual strength together in Christ was greater than any foe they faced. Even in times of war, they did not forsake gathering together. Second, they took the Word of God into their hearts in an active way— knowing God would bless them when the principles of their faith were reflected in their behavior.

The strength and courage Haille discovered in the people of Le Chambon was a result of their simple obedience to God—never to stop meeting together to worship and hear His Word. When extreme difficulty came their way, their unity in the faith was a habitual part of their everyday lives.

Thank God today for a church where you can receive strength and courage. If you don't go to church, ask the Lord to lead you to the body of believers just right for you.

The Believer's Position

Your life is hidden with Christ in God.
COLOSSIANS 3:3 NKJV

The story is told of a sheriff who decided it was time to tighten the performance standards for his deputies. Each deputy had to re-qualify on the firing range and pass tougher requirements. The target was moved farther away, from fifteen yards to twenty-five yards, and the deputies were required to fire off twelve shots in eighteen seconds.

The day before trials, Deputy George Burgin was fitted with his first pair of trifocals. George got ready for his shoot and drew a bead on the target to help his aim.

"Suddenly," he said, "I began to perspire. And when I perspire, my glasses fog up. There I was with a bead drawn on the target, and all I could see was fog.

"Then I remembered what our old Navy instructor had taught us: 'If (for some reason) you ever lose sight of the target,' he said, 'just remember your position.'

"So, I just held my position and pulled the trigger as last as I could. By then I had less than eighteen seconds, but I fired all twelve shots. When I took off my glasses and wiped them, I discovered I had hit the bullseye every time."[18]

Sometimes circumstances may cause us to lose sight of our target, or our goal. We do not have a clear sense of where we are headed. If that's the case, we need to do what Deputy Burgin did and remember our position. As Christians, we are securely positioned "in Christ."

Each day we must choose to orient ourselves and face the challenges of the day—whatever they may be. We have the choice to approach the days opportunities with eager optimism born of faith. When we do, nothing can happen to make us lose sight of our goal. "Positioned" in Christ, we cannot miss!

———————————————

As To The Lord

With good will render service, as to the Lord, and not to men.
EPHESIANS 6:7 NASB

When we think of the most noble professions, we nearly always think of those that offer a service, such as doctors, lawyers, or teachers. Perhaps at the pinnacle of the service professions are those who are involved in full-time ministry — the helping of others in their spiritual lives in the name of the Lord. We tend to revere most highly those who make a commitment to serving God and others: pastors, priests, monks, missionaries, evangelists, and Bible teachers.

Ministry, however, is not limited to those who earn their living by it. Ministry is the call and challenge of God to all Christians. Ministry is giving to others and living our lives *as unto the Lord.*

Ministry happens in the home, in the school, on the street, at the grocery store, in the boardroom, at the committee meeting, and in the gym. It happens wherever and whenever a person, motivated by the love of Jesus Christ, performs an act of loving service for another person.

Gandhi once wrote:

"If when we plunge our hand into a bowl of water,

Or stir up the fire with the bellows

Or tabulate interminable columns of figures on our bookkeeping table,

Or, burnt by the sun, we are plunged in the mud of the rice field.

Or standing by the smelter's furnace

We do not fulfill the same religious life as if in prayer in a monastery, the world will never be saved." [19]

There is no ignoble work except that which is void of ministry! There is no lack of meaning in any job performed with Gods love and "as unto the Lord."

Whatever the tasks you face today, perform them as if you were performing them for Jesus Himself, because ultimately you are!

———————————————————

The Critical Difference

Blessed are von when people insult you, persecute you and falsely say all kinds of evil against you because of me. Rejoice and be glad, because great is your reward in heaven, for in the same way they persecuted the prophets who were before you.
MATTHEW 5:11-12

It was built for an international exposition in the last century and called "monstrous" by both critics and citizens. They loudly demanded the structure be torn down as soon as the 1889 exposition closed. Yet from the moment its architect first conceived the structure, he took pride in it and loyally defended it. He knew it was destined for greatness.

Today it stands as one of the architectural wonders of the modern world. It has become the primary landmark of Paris, France. The architect, of course, was Alexander Gustave Eiffel. His famous structure? The Eiffel Tower.

Jesus Christ was loyal to another structure—the Church. He entrusted the building of the Church to an unlikely band of disciples, whom He defended, prayed for, and prepared to take the Gospel to the far-reaching corners of the world. To outsiders, the disciples of Jesus probably had a reputation as ignorant, politically weak, religiously untrained, disorganized, and in moments, blundering idiots. But Jesus, the architect of the Church, knew His structure was destined for greatness.

Being a Christian has never been "politically correct." Critics through the years have compiled a list of derogatory names to call the Church and its members. In spite of criticism, however, we are instructed to carry on. We are to persist in building the body of Christ until His return. As we build, we can be assured we will please God and He will bless us.

The famous Finnish composer Jean Sibelius once consoled a young musician who had received a bad review by saying, "Remember, son, there is no city in the world where they have erected a statue to a critic."

Jesus said, "I will build my church; and the gates of hell will not prevail against it" (Matthew 16:18). One day the Church will be the ones left standing. What will the critics say then?

No matter what comes your way today, be proud you are a member of Jesus' Church!

On a Weekday Morning

Let me hear of your steadfast love in the morning, for in you
I put my trust. Teach me the way I should go, for to you I lift
up my soul.
PSALM 143:8 NRSV

Regular, frequent prayer is an important part of the lives of people who desire a meaningful relationship with God. John Wesley, a devout Christian and the founder of Methodism, had a deep concern for the "state of his soul." Because of that concern he regularly prayed two hours a day. Here is one of John Wesleys prayers, which you may want to include in your devotions:

"O God, who are the giver of all good gifts, I your unworthy servant entirely desire to praise your name for all the expressions of your bounty toward me. Blessed be your love for giving your Son to die for our sins, for the means of grace, and for the hope of glory. Blessed be your love for all the temporal benefits which you have with a liberal hand poured out upon me; for my health and strength, food and

raiment, and all other necessaries . . . I also bless you, that after all my refusals of your grace, you still have patience with me, have preserved me this night, and given me yet another day to renew and perfect my repentance.

"Make yourself always present to my mind, and let your love will and rule my soul, in all those places, and companies, and employments to which you call me this day. O you who are good and do good, who extend your loving-kindness to all mankind, the work of your hands, your image, capable of knowing and loving you eternally: suffer me to exclude none, O Lord, from my charity, who are the objects of your mercy; but let me treat all my neighbors with the tender love which is due to your servants and to your children. Let your love to me, O blessed Saviour, be the pattern of my love to them.

"Preserve my parents, my brothers and sisters, my friends and relations, and all mankind in their souls and bodies. Forgive mv enemies, and in your due time make them kindly affected toward me. O grant that we, with those who are already dead in your faith and fear, may together partake of a joyful resurrection."[20]

———————————————

Love Your Enemies

How good and pleasant it is when brothers live together in unity!

PSALM 133:1

With the Cold War over, Americans and Russians seem to be looking at each other in a new way. Imagine being an American soldier stationed in Bosnia-Herzegovina, working alongside your Russian counterparts. How do you work together after decades of mistrust?

American and Russian officers who were asked this question agreed that when it comes right down to it, people are people, and soldiers are soldiers. When there's a goal to reach, one finds a way to communicate. The mission is kept in focus, ground rules are established, language barriers are overcome, mutual interests are discovered, and before long, friendships develop!

The early Christian believers certainly thought they had an enemy in Saul of Tarsus, and the feeling was mutual. Saul was extremely active in persecuting Christians in Jerusalem and was determined to deal the same harsh blows to believers in Damascus. But then Jesus appeared to him and his life was dramatically changed.

Believers in Damascus were suspicious of Saul when he arrived and declared he was also a believer in Jesus Christ. But as they witnessed his manner of living God dramatically changed their hearts. In the end, the apostle *Paul* became an ardent friend of believers everywhere.

Have you secretly been at "war" with a co-worker or neighbor? Beginning today make a concerted effort to find common ground with that person. Smile when your instincts tell you to grimace. Stay focused on your goals and stick to the ground rules when working or volunteering together. Talk to them. Seek out hobbies, concerns, or family interests you hold in common. Start treating the person as you would a friend, not an enemy. After all, it's when your enemy is no longer your enemy that the fun begins!

The Bible says to love your enemies and pray for those who despitefully use you, and in doing so you heap coals upon their heads. (See Romans 12:20.) The coals are blessings! When you sow blessings you reap blessings!

Which Lifestyle?

For God so loved the world, that He gave . . .
JOHN 3:16 NASB

The word "lifestyle" has been popular for several decades. In simplest terms, this word denotes how we live from a financial standpoint, the possessions we choose to buy and how much money we have to spend.

A great deal is being written these days about the simple life—downshifting or downscaling. At the same time, we see an ongoing exaltation in our culture of all that is "excessive." As a nation, we seem to love peering into the lifestyles of the rich and famous. We envy them. Every few minutes television commercials tell us to buy more and better possessions.

The two paths—one toward a materially leaner life and the other toward a materially fatter life—are like opposite lanes on a highway. We are going either in one direction or the other. We are seeking to discard and downsize, or to acquire and add.

The Scriptures call us to neither a Spartan nor an opulent lifestyle, but rather, to a lifestyle of *generosity*—

a life without greed or hoarding. A life of giving freely, a life of putting everything we have at Gods disposal. Our lifestyle is not about how much we earn, what we own, or where we travel and reside. It's *how* we relate to other people and how willing we are to share all we have with them.

In *Visions of a World Hungry*, Thomas G. Pettepiece offers this prayer: "Lord, help me choose a simpler lifestyle that promotes solidarity with the worlds poor . . . affords greater opportunity to work together with my neighbors."

As you touch your various possessions throughout the day—from the appliances in your home to your clothing and your vehicle—ask yourself, "Would I be willing to loan, give, or share this with other people?" Then ask the even tougher question, "Do I actually share, loan, or give of my substance on a regular basis to others?"

Perfect Combination

You are the salt of the earth. But if the salt loses its saltiness, how can it be made salty again? It is no longer good for anything, except to be thrown out and trampled by men.
MATTHEW 5:1,3

———————————

Sodium is an extremely active element which always links itself to another element.
Chlorine is a poisonous gas.

When combined, chlorine stabilizes sodium and sodium neutralizes the poison of the chlorine.

The result, sodium chloride, is common table salt, a highly stable substance used through the centuries to preserve meat, enhance flavor and, prior to modern medicine, help clean and heal wounds.

For a Christian, love and truth can be like sodium and chlorine. Both are essential elements in a believers life, but pursuing one without the other can be unmanageable and even dangerous.

Love without truth is flighty, sometimes blind, and often willing to combine with strange or perverse doctrines. It is highly unstable, tossed to and fro on a sea of emotions.

On the other hand, truth by itself can be offensive, sometimes even poisonous. Spoken without love, it can turn people away from God. It can wound, even kill, a person's longing for the nurturing presence of the Heavenly Father.

When truth and love are combined in an individual or a church, however, we have what Jesus called "the salt of the earth." We are able to heal those with spiritual wounds, preserve and encourage the best in one another, and bring out the personal zest and unique gifts of each person.

Today as you deal with others, seek to let your words and actions be *grounded in truth* and *delivered with love.*

Leaving a Legacy

*My heart is steadfast, O God; I will sing and make music
with all my soul.*
P S A L M   1 0 8 : 1

W illiam Congreve said, "Music alone
with sudden charms can bind the
wand'ring sense, and calm the troubled
mind." Walter Turnbull, founder of the Boys Choir of
Harlem, would add that music can also change the life
of a child.

The success of Turnbull's work is well documented.
An astounding ninety-eight percent of his choir
members finish high school and go on to college. More
important, they benefit from Turnbull's teachings. A
healthy dose of old-fashioned values is mixed in with
the music he teaches—the kind of values Turnbull
learned as a child in rural Mississippi.

He believes America's sense of community is
slipping away, and he hopes to impress upon his choir
members the importance of nurturing one another to
excel. For twenty-six years, Turnbull has demonstrated
this principle to his students by taking them around

the world—to Europe, Japan, Canada, and the Caribbean. With a current roster of 450 boys and girls, eight to eighteen years old, that's no small feat. But numbers and age do not matter to Turnbull. Character does. His satisfaction comes from knowing that his choir members are learning to be better people.

Most of us would love to leave the kind of legacy Walter Turnbull is leaving to the world. What w'e need to recognize is that Turnbull didn't create his 450-member choir in a day. He started where he was with a small group of neighborhood kids in a church basement. He didn't have money for choir robes or music. But he did have a desire to introduce those children to the joy of music.

Do what you can, where you are, with the people God has placed in your path right now, today. Regardless of how you help others, you will put a song in their hearts.

———————————————

Leader of the Pack

See, the former things have taken place, and new things I declare; before they spring into being I announce them to you.
ISAIAH 42:9

Being the owner of a small business is not easy. Just when you start to build a clientele, along comes a crafty competitor who copies your style or improves on your methods. Next thing you know, revenues are falling and you find yourself looking over your shoulder, trying to avoid being hit by another wave of wanna-be's.

A man on the West Coast found himself in this situation. His first venture was commercial fishing. When larger companies took over the water, he began renting out small sailboats and kayaks to people who wanted to explore the bay. Soon others with stronger financial backing moved in on that business.

Once again, he needed a new idea.

How about submarine tours? After doing some research, the entrepreneur realized the cost of buying and maintaining a sub was beyond his reach. But a semi-submersible underwater viewing boat was not! The boat looks like a sub. but it doesn't dive. Passengers can go below deck and view the fascinating world under the sea.[21]

When your income seems to be going out with the tide, you may need to be a little creative. Talk with other people, do some research, consider even the "crazy" ideas and glean what you can from them. You never know which wave might be the one that carries you safely and profitably to the shore.

God's creative work didn't end with His creation of the world. He continues His work today by giving each of us a dose of creativity. He invites us to be part of His plan and purpose for the earth by using this creative energy. Your ideas are God's gift to you for your provision, prosperity, and the fulfillment of your purpose in life.

Ask the Lord to inspire you anew today. Ask Him to give you His next *idea* for your life!

Feeding the Poor

Blessed are the poor in spirit, for theirs is the kingdom of heaven.
MATTHEW 5:3 NASB

O ne day a young executive was asked to share with his fellow employees how he felt about participating in the company's voluntary "feeding the poor" program. He took one early morning slot each week to ladle soup and pass out sandwiches to nearly 400 homeless and street people in his city. The young man said this:

"I go on Tuesdays to feed those we call poor, and in fact, they are poor in material things. Some of them are poor in many ways, and we also try to help them with encouragement, advice, and on occasion, a word of prayer. But in many ways, these hungry and poor men and women have nurtured something in me – they have made me more aware of the spiritual side of my life and they have led me to be aware that we all 'feed' each other in many ways every day – either good nourishment for the soul, or poison.

"I have a new understanding that when I go home and genuinely compliment my wife, or sit down to read a story to

mv daughter, or toss a ball with mv son, I am feeding something inside them. I no longer see myself as part of the Tuesday-morning feeding team, but as a 24-hour-a-day feeding volunteer."

Who will you feed today?

And what will you feed them?

Mother Teresa wrote in *A Gift for God*, "People are hungry for something more beautiful, for something greater than people round about can give. There is a great hunger for God in the world today. Everywhere there is much suffering, but there is also great hunger for God and love for each other."

Today you will encounter people who are *hungry*—outwardly and inwardly. God has equipped you in unique ways to "feed" them with natural food as well as His Word, His love, and His presence. He invites you to volunteer to participate in *His* feeding program.

———————————

Bearing Fruit

Meditate upon these things; give thyself wholly to them; that thy profiting may appear to all.
1 TIMOTHY 4:15 KJV

Two brothers were out walking on their lather's vast acreage when they came upon a peach tree, its branches heavy with fruit. Each brother ate several juicy, tree-ripened peaches.

When they started toward the house, one brother gathered enough peaches for a delicious peach cobbler and several jars of jam. The second brother cut a limb from the tree to start a new peach tree. When he got home he carefully tended the tree-cutting until he could plant it outdoors. The branch took root and eventually produced healthy crops of peaches for him to enjoy year after year.

The Bible is like the fruit-bearing tree. Hearing the Word of God is like the first brother. He gathered fruit from hearing the Word and had enough to take home with him to eat later. But that doesn't compare with having your own peach tree in the backyard.

Memorizing the Word is like having the fruit tree in your backyard. It is there to nourish you all the time.

Scripture memorization is often considered a dull, burdensome task. But we could gel highly motivated if we were given one hundred dollars for every Bible verse we memorized! The rewards of Scripture memory may not always be monetary, but they are a far better treasure for life.

One of the greatest values of Scripture memory is that it keeps us from sin. In Psalm 119:11 (NKJV) the psalmist wrote: "Your word I have hidden in my heart, that I might not sin against You."

For many people, the morning is the best time to memorize Scripture because one's mind is fresh, alert, and free from distractions. There are many different ways to memorize Scripture. Find the one that works best for you and begin hiding God's Word in your heart so it may bring *continual* life and nourishment to you. This will produce fruit in your life which you can share with others.

Setting the Stage for Success

Do not be terrified; do not be discouraged, for the Lord your God will be with you wherever you go.
JOSHUA 1:9

A promising singer faced a big audition. Alone in a hotel room far from home, she was excited about the opportunity, but was also afraid of failing. *If I don't get this job,* she told herself. *I'll probably never get another audition.*

You may have felt that same way before a job interview, thinking that if you didn't get the job, you might never find another. All of us occasionally fall into the pit of discouragement. We simply can't see any option other than the one before us. Here's how the singer dug her way out of this thinking.

On the day of her audition she picked up a magazine at breakfast and read a story about Garry Kasparov, a great Soviet chess player. He had been involved in a months-long match with Anatoly Karpov, the world champion. Kasparov was losing, but he didn't cave in. He fought hard, regained lost ground, and eventually won the match.

The young singer was inspired. *If he could do it, so can I!* she thought. Confidently, she walked onto the stage that afternoon and sang her heart out. That audition led to the first of many jobs. New life was breathed into her career.

Its easy to lose faith in your ability to succeed. But if you look around, you'll find someone else who has triumphed against the odds. Even if you can't find a living example of a failure-reversing or difficulty-overcoming hero in your circle of acquaintances, you can certainly find one in the Scriptures.

The Bible is filled with stories of men and women who faced seemingly insurmountable odds and came through *with Gods help*. Allow that persons example to inspire you. The same God who helped them is present and wants to help you now.

Whose Will?

Not as I will, but as Thou wilt.
MATTHEW 26:39 NASB

A Christian woman once confided to a friend that she found it nearly impossible to pray, "Thy will be done." She was afraid of what the Lord might call her to do. Very specifically, she feared being called to a snake-infested swamp to take the Gospel to head-hunting natives. As the mother of a young child, she simply could not bear the thought that God might call her to leave her child and sacrifice her life on the mission field.

Her friend said to her, "Suppose your little girl came to you tomorrow morning and said, 'Mommy, I have made up my mind to let you have your own way with me from now on. I'm always going to obey you and I trust you completely to do everything you think is best for me'? How would you feel?"

The woman replied, "Why, I'd feel wonderful. I'd shower her with hugs and kisses and do everything in my power to give her all the things that were good for her and which would help her find her talents and use them to their fullest."

The friend said, "Well, that's how the Lord feels as your Heavenly Father. His will is going to be far better than anything you have imagined, not far worse."

God's will for Jesus did not end with the pain and suffering of the Cross. The "end" of Gods will for Jesus was His glorious resurrection from the dead, His ascension to Heaven, His being seated at the right hand of the Father, and His exaltation as the King of kings and Lord of lords forever!

As Hannah Whitall Smith wrote, "Better and sweeter than health, or friends, or money, or fame, or ease, or prosperity, is the adorable will of our God. It gilds the darkest hours with a divine halo, and sheds brightest sunshine on the gloomiest paths . . . it is only a glorious privilege."

Make your prayer today, "Thy will be done, Lord." And then see what *good* things God has for you to experience!

Remembering God

Choose for yourselves this day whom you will serve.
J O S H U A   2 4 : 1 5

A rabbi once summoned the townsfolk to meet in the square for an important announcement. The merchants resented having to leave their businesses. The farmers could scarcely see how they could leave their fields. The housewives protested against leaving their chores. But obedient to the call of their spiritual leader, the townspeople gathered together to hear the announcement their teacher felt was so important to make at that time.

The rabbi said, "I wish to announce that there is a God in the world." And with that, he departed.

The people stood in silence—stunned, but not bewildered. They understood what he had said, with an understanding born of a heartfelt conviction. They realized they had been acting as if God did *not* exist. While they observed rituals and recited the correct order of prayers, their actions did not comply with the commandments of God. Their daily bread was sought and taken with little thought and reverence for God.

We may not openly deny God, but we try to confine Him to some remote corner of life. We keep Him away from our daily doings, associations, obligations, experiences, joys, heartaches, and all the commonplace things required to keep body and soul together. The fact is, however:

- *There is a God in the world you call your neighborhood.*
- *There is a God in the world you call Your workplace.*
- *There is a God in the offices you frequent, the hospitals you visit, the airports through which you travel, the shops in which you make your purchases, and the dozens of places you walk in the course of a week.*

There is a God . . . and He wants to be a part of everything you do.

Recognize He is with you *wherever* you go today. The knowledge that He is with you and that He is interested in every detail of your life will bring joy and peace to every experience.

———————————————————

Precious Ones

*Since thou wast precious in my sight, thou hast been
honorable, and I have loved thee.*
ISAIAH 43:4

A young woman named June volunteered
at a church agency that served the poor
and homeless of her city. One day June
met George, who had come in to get some help. Winter
was coming and he needed a jacket and some shoes to
help keep him warm.

He took a seat in the chapel, because the waiting
room was crowded and noisy. When he indicated he
wanted a Bible, June went to get one for him while he
waited his turn in the clothing room. When she
returned with a Bible, she sat down to talk with him for
awhile.

George looked like he was in his late 50s or early
60s. His thin hair was beginning to gray. Deep lines
marked his face. His hands were stiff and he had lost
part of one finger. It was 1:30 in the afternoon, and he
smelled slightly of alcohol. He was a short, slight man,
and he spoke softly. He had come into the agency

alone, and June wondered if he had any family — or anyone who knew or cared that he existed.

June wrote Georges name in the front of his Bible along with the date. Then she showed him the study helps in the back which would help him find key passages.

As they talked, the thought occurred to June: *George is one of God's very precious creatures.* She wondered it George knew. She wondered how long it had been since someone had told him. What if he had never been told he was precious to God — and to all Gods other children as well?

George had very little influence or stature, but God spoke to June through him that day, "My children need to know they are precious to Me. Please tell them that." Since then she has made that message a part of every encounter she has at the church agency.

Ask the Lord how you might share the message, "You are precious to God," with others today through your words and actions.

———————————————

On a Wing and a Prayer

If the Lord delights in a man's way, he makes his steps firm;
though he stumble, he will not fall.
P S A L M   3 7 : 2 3 - 2 4

---

fledge (verb) 1. of a bird: to acquire the feathers necessary for
flight

Perhaps it's been a couple of decades, or maybe only a couple of years, since you officially "left the nest." Your destination may have been college, a job, or marriage. If your parents were like most, they no doubt were excited, sad, and terrified—all at the same time—at the prospect of your leaving their protective care.

Biologists can relate to those parental feelings, especially when it comes to peregrine falcons. In this day and age, they are as likely to build their nests on bridges and skyscrapers as on cliffs. When falcon chicks "fledge" in an urban area, they have less room to take practice flights and so their first official flight is sometimes their last. Wires, windows, streets, and sidewalks can be unforgiving landing pads.[23]

To a biologist whose job it is to track these wonderful birds, each lost chick is a devastating blow. However, the chicks will die if they don't attempt flight, and eventually that would mean extinction for the falcons. Risk holds the possibility of failure, but not to risk would mean certain death.

We humans often spend years preparing ourselves for the future, earning degrees, practicing our craft, seeking out opportunities. But eventually the day comes when we have to face the world, including the possibility for failure.

The thought that we may not succeed at our chosen endeavor shouldn't keep us from spreading our wings. Not only is our own future at stake, but from a much broader perspective, the future growth and development of the human race is involved. Our contribution, even if small, is part of a much greater whole.

As Christians, we must live adventures in faith for ourselves and to further the kingdom of God. However, as children of God, we may falter momentarily, but God assures us of ultimate victory.

If you stumble or make a mistake today, remember Who is there to set you back on your feet and get you going again. God has a wonderful, exciting plan for your life (See Jeremiah 29:11) and as long as you follow Him, there is nothing you can do to mess it up!

The Big Picture

I go to prepare a place for you. And if I go and prepare a
place for you, I will come again and receive you to Myself;
that where I am, there you may be also.
JOHN 14:2-3 NKJV

During War II, parachutes were constructed by the thousands in factories across the United States. From the workers point of view, the job was tedious. It required stitching endless lengths of colorless fabric, crouched over a sewing machine eight to ten hours a day. The result of a days work was a formless, massive heap of cloth that had no visible resemblance to a parachute.

To keep the workers motivated and concerned with quality, the management in one factory held a meeting with its workers each morning. The workers were told approximately how many parachutes had been strapped onto the backs of pilots, copilots, and other "flying" personnel the previous day. They knew just how many men had jumped to safety from disabled planes. The managers encouraged their workers to see the "big picture" of their job.

As a second means of motivation, the workers were asked to form a mental picture of a husband, brother, or son who might be the one saved by the parachute they were sewing.

The level of quality in that factory was one of the highest on record![24]

Don't let the tedium of each days chores and responsibilities wear you down so you only see the "stitching" in front of you. Keep your eyes on the big picture. Focus on *why* you do what you do and who will benefit from your work, including those you don't know and may never meet. You may not have all the answers to the question, "Why am I here?" but you can rest assured, the Lord does!

Ultimately, the Bible tells us we will be in heaven for eternity — and that is the biggest picture of all! God is preparing us for heaven, just as He is preparing heaven for us. He is creating us to be the people He wants to live with forever.

Whatever mundane tasks or trivial pursuits you undertake today, see them in the light of eternity. They will take on a whole new meaning!

———————————————

The Sky's the Limit

For my yokes is easy, and my burden is light.
M A T T H E W   1 1 : 3 0   K J V

People are often afraid that commitment to Jesus Christ means an endless list of "don'ts" and "thou shalt nots."

Highly motivated personalities are especially vulnerable to the lie that Gods ways will restrict their creativity and growth. They fear they may never reach their full potential if they are tied to a lot of religious restrictions.

Sadly, some of the smartest people on earth will never reach their lull potential because they *aren't* tied to Jesus. The same holds for those who see His commands as "taking away all their fun." The fact is, true and lasting joy comes through knowing Jesus and following Him.

Consider this: You have watched a kite fly in the wind. Would you say the string that holds it is burdensome? No, it is there to control the kite. The kite will not fly unless it is in partnership with the string. The string and the kite are yoked together. You cannot cut the string and expect the kite to soar right up into the heavens. When the restrictive yoke of the string is cut, the kite may seem to fly freely for a moment, but it w ill soon crash to the ground.

The string gives the kite direction and purpose by sustaining its position against the wind and using the wind to its advantage. Without the string, the kite would be at the mercy of every passing influence and would doubtless end up being trapped in a tree or falling to the ground. When it is time for the kite to come to earth, the string gently reels it in, safely missing tree limbs and telephone poles.

In like manner, our daily surrender to the Lord Jesus is not burdensome, nor does it take away enjoyment in life. Like the kite string, He makes certain the wind is in our favor and we are always in position to get the most out of life.

Let Jesus be your "kite string" today, and see if you don't fly higher!

Taproots

*The Almighty . . . blesses you with blessings of the heavens
above [and] blessings of the deep that lies below.*
GENESIS 49:25

T he art of raising miniature trees, known as
bonsai, was developed by the Japanese. To
create a miniature tree, the taproot is cut,
forcing the tree to live on only the nourishment
provided by the little roots growing along the surface
of the soil. The tree lives, but it does not grow. Trees
dwarfed in this way reach a height of only twelve to
eighteen inches.

The taproot of a tree is the part of the root system
that goes deep into the soil to absorb essential minerals
and huge quantities of water—sometimes several
hundred quarts a day. Taproots grow deepest in dry,
sandy areas where there is little rainfall. The root
system of a tree not only nourishes the tree but
provides stability, anchoring it securely into the ground
so it cannot be blown over by strong winds.

The root system is a good analogy for the Christian
life. Richard J. Foster wrote, "Superficiality is the curse

of our age . . . The desperate need today is not for a greater number of intelligent people, or gifted people, but for deep people."

How do Christians grow deep in their spiritual life? In the same way a taproot grows deep—in search of the nourishment that will cause it to grow. In modern culture, Christians have to seek out spiritual food that will result in spiritual maturity. Regular times of prayer and Bible study, individual and corporate worship, serving others, and Christian fellowship are just some of the ways Christians can grow deep roots.

What are the benefits of depth in our spiritual life? Like the tree . . .

- *we will be able to stand strong—"the righteous cannot be uprooted" (Proverbs 12:3), and*
- *we will be fruitful—"the root of the righteous flourishes" (Proverbs 12:12).*

Seek the Lord daily, so you can grow *deep* in your faith and withstand the storms of life.

———————————

A New Day

Old things have passed away; behold, all things have become new.
2 CORINTHIANS 5:17 NKJV

I n the early morning, the day lies before us as a pure canvas to be painted. Its hours have not yet been tainted with sweat, suffering, sorrow, or sighing. They have not been marred with tears or blood. Neither have they been polluted by worry, frustration, or conflict. Nor punctuated by shouts, screams, or cries. The day laid out before us holds only promise and potential!

Imagine yourself for a moment standing in a mountain forest by a clear lake, with a dark blue sky overhead and the warm glow of the sun, just beginning to burn away the fog rising from the water. In such a moment, the world appears to be asleep—there is a natural stillness that speaks of purity and strength.

So too with us. We are at our purest and strongest early in the morning. It is then that we should ask the Lord to keep us that way for the remainder of the day. Mary S. Edgar captures this idea in the hymn, "God,

Who Touchest Earth with Beauty." Make it your song today:

God, who touchest earth with beauty.
Make mv heart anew;
With thy spirit recreate me.
Pure and strong and true.
Like thy springs and running waters
Make me crystal pure:
Like thy rocks of lowering grandeur
Make me strong and sure.
Like thy dancing waves in sunlight
Make me glad and free;
Like the straightness of the pine trees
Let me upright he.
Like the arching of the heavens
Lift my thoughts above;
Turn my dreams to noble action.
Ministries of love.
God. who touchest earth with beauty.
Make my heart anew:
Keep me ever, by thy spirit,
Pure and strong and true. Amen[25]

_____

Watch Where You're Goin'!

Do you not know that in a race all the runners run, but only one gets the prize? Run in such a way as to get the prize.
1 CORINTHIANS 9:24

On March 6, 1987, Eamon Coughlan, the Irish world record holder in the 1,500 meter, was competing in a qualifying heat at the World Indoor Track Championships in Indianapolis. With only two and a hall laps left, he was accidentally tripped by another runner. Coughlan crashed onto the track, but with great effort managed to gel up, shake off the blow to his body, and regain his stride. With an explosive burst of effort, he managed to catch the leaders. Amazingly, with only twenty yards left in the race, he was in third place, a position good enough for him to qualify for the finals.

Just then, Coughlan looked over his shoulder to the inside. When he didn't see anyone he slowed his stride. To his great surprise another runner, charging hard on the outside, passed him only a yard before the finish line, thus eliminating him from the final race. Coughlan's great comeback effort was rendered worthless because he took his eyes off the finish line and assumed that his race would be run without further challenge.

Today you will face many distractions that have the potential to take your attention away from your goals. Some of those distractions will be of the small bump-in-the-road variety — minor, quickly-overcome annoyances along your path.

Others may be of the stumble-and-fall variety — those that seriously threaten your progress if you don't pick yourself up and move on. But the distraction that most seriously threatens your goal is the one that looks as if it is no threat at all: the I've-got-it-made-so-relax variety. It compels you to look over your shoulder, slow your pace, and take your eyes off the finish line.

The advice you were given early in life is still applicable today: Watch where you're goin'!

───────────────────────

Which Day Planner?

The things that I purpose, do I purpose according to the flesh?
2 CORINTHIANS 1:17 KJV

One of the challenges of our busy lives today is to be organized, so we can "get it all done." There are a number of organizers and calendars available to help us schedule the precious hours of the day. Beepers and mobile telephones give us instant communication with anyone anywhere. We no longer get away from it all, because now we can take it all with us!

Sometimes we need to be challenged not to "get it all done," but to slow down and reflect on what it is we are trying to accomplish. We must be sure we are headed in the right direction with our families, our work, our church, our community, and our personal lives.

If we are not careful and prayerful, we may find ourselves agreeing with the modern-day philosopher who noted, "So what if you win the rat race—you are still a rat!"

God has a different "daily planner." The psalmist wrote about it in Psalm 105:

- *Give thanks to the Lord.*
- *Call on His name.*
- *Make known among the nations what he has done.*
- *Sing to him, sing praise to him.*
- *Tell of all his wonderful acts.*
- *Glory in his holy name.*
- *Let the hearts of those who seek the Lord rejoice.*
- *Look to the Lord and his strength.*
- *Seek his face always.*
- *Remember the wonders he has done, his miracles, and the judgments he has pronounced.*

Each day we have the privilege of consulting with the King of kings and Lord of lords to determine what path we will take, what tasks are most important, and who needs us the most.

Every Little Bit Helps

He who began a good work in you will carry it on to completion.
P H I L I P P I A N S   1 : 6

C an the dead be raised in todays world? It all depends on what has died. Sometimes bringing something to life is simply a matter of hard work and time . . . perhaps even centuries. The stall at Redwood National Park in California will tell you that attempting to do this is definitely worth the effort.

In 1978, the park "grew" by sixty square miles of clearcut forest. Congress gave the park's managers a challenge: restore the land to its natural state. A warning was also given: the final results of your work won't be visible for hundreds of years.

Work began. Since 1978, roads have been removed, stream and estuary habitats have been repaired, land that was stripped of vegetation has been replanted, and hundreds of haul roads and ski trails have been erased. In the process, the park has become something of a "living laboratory," a means of helping environmental researchers learn more about restoration ecology. What they have learned so far at Redwood has been beneficial to managing the health of other national and state parks.[26]

The next time you think your efforts may be too little too late, remember the worlds tallest tree — located at Redwood — did not grow to be 368 feet high overnight, it takes time to become magnificent.

The Scriptures do not tell us to be restored to our "natural" state, but to be transformed into the image of Christ Jesus. (See Romans 12:2.) This transformation isn't immediate. Some habits and patterns take a long time to change. Hurtful memories require healing, and may never be fully erased. New ways of thinking and responding can be slow to develop.

However, our transformation is the work of the Holy Spirit within us, and He never fails! Trust God today to be at work in your transformation — a project that may take all your lifetime and be complete only in eternity, but will end in your wholeness.

A Shared Vision

The Lord has been mindful of us; He will bless us . . . He will
bless those who fear the land, both small and great.
P S A L M   1 1 5 : 1 2 - 1 3   N K J V

I n *The Reasons of the Heart*, John S. Dunne writes
eloquently:

"'*There is a dream dreaming us,*' *a Bushman once*
told Laurens Van der Post. We are part of a dream,
according to him, part of a vision. What is more, we can
become aware of it. Although we are far removed from the
Bushmen and their vision, it seems we can indeed come to a
sense of being dreamed, being seen, being known. Our
mind's desire is to know, to understand; but our heart's
desire is intimacy, to be known, to be understood. To see God
with our mind would be to know God, to understand God;
but to see God with our heart would be to have a sense of
being known by God, of being understood by God."

"*If there is a dream dreaming us, it will he God's vision*
of us, and if we have a sense of being part of that dream, it
will he our heart's vision of God."[27]

As we explore and encounter Gods dream for us
we find our clearest and highest sense of identity and

purpose in life, which gives us motivation and direction for each day.

Do you have a sense of Gods vision for your life today? How does He see you? What does He desire for you? What does He dream of your doing, becoming, and being?

We know from His Word that God desires for you to be a person of character and quality, a person of noble and uncompromising virtue, a person of strength and spiritual power. He is calling you to a close, personal, and intimate relationship with Him. He eagerly desires to entrust you with His plans and desires for your life.

God has given you specific talents, abilities, spiritual gifts, and material endowments which He longs for you to use to their fullest. Purpose in your heart today to be His friend, His child, His heir, so that He can do what He loves to do — reward you with even greater blessings.

———————————————

Perspective

I have become all things to all men so that by all possible means I might save some.
1 CORINTHIANS 9:22

E ven though God gives us a brand-new day every twenty-four hours, we seldom begin it with a brand-new outlook. All too often, we regard the day ahead as "just another day," We may see a different date, but the day seems filled with the same routine, same troubles, same faces, same responsibilities.

Wouldn't it be wonderful if we could look at each day from a slightly different perspective and, with Gods guidance, learn to serve Him better as a result?

A Bible translator named Fraiser learned the importance of different perspectives in a very interesting way. Known simply as "Fraiser of Lisuland" in northern Burma, he translated the Scriptures into the Lisu language. Fraiser went on to do translation work somewhere else for a time, leaving a young fellow with the task of teaching the people to read.

When he returned six months later, he found three students and the teacher seated around a table, the Scriptures open in front of the teacher. Fraiser was amazed to see that as each of the students read for him, he left the Bible where it was — in front of him. The man on the left read it sideways, the man on the right read it sideways but from the other side, and the man across from the teacher read it upside down. Since they had always occupied the same chairs, they each had learned to read from that particular perspective, and they each thought that was how their language was written!

We can be like that too. When we learn something from only one perspective, we may think that its the only perspective. We have the solution to our problem, but nobody else's. Sometimes its necessary to change seats and assume a different perspective on the same truth in order to help others.

The principles of truth in God's Word never change, but our understanding of them does! Ask God to give you new insights about Him today. With your new perspective, you may see the solution to a problem that has plagued someone for years.

As our perspective broadens, our ability to help ourselves and others increases.

Downhill from Here

But ye are a chosen generation, a royal priesthood, an holy
nation, a peculiar people; that ye should show forth the
praises of him who hath called you out of darkness into his
marvelous light.
1 PETER 2:9

J ean-Claude Killy, the French ski champion, did
more than work hard at his sport.

When he made his nations ski team in the early
1960s, he was determined to be the best. He
decided vigorous training was the key. Up at dawn
each day, he ran up mountains with his skis on — a very
painful activity. Weight training, sprinting . . . Killy was
determined to do whatever it took to reach peak
physical condition.

Other team members were working just as hard,
and in the end it was a change in style, not
conditioning, that set Killy apart.

The goal in ski racing is to ski down a prescribed
mountain course faster than anyone else. Killy began
experimenting to see if he could pare any seconds off
his time. He found that if he skied with his legs apart,

he had better balance. He also found that if he sat back on his skis when executing a turn, instead of leaning forward as was customary, he had better control, which also resulted in faster times. Rather than regarding his ski poles as an accessory for balance, Killy tried using them to propel him forward.

Killy's style was unorthodox. But when he won most of the major ski events in 1966 and 1967, including three gold medals at the Winter Olympics, skiers around the world took notice. Today, the Killy style is the norm among downhill and slalom racers. Any other "style" would be considered odd.[28]

As Christians we are not called to conform to the world's standards, but to God's standards. Our lifestyle should challenge people to come to Jesus Christ and live according to His higher ways and purposes. The Christian "style" may seem odd to the unbeliever, but in the end, it is the style that will prevail!

Don't be afraid to be a little "unusual" today in the eyes of those who observe you. Your example may help win them over to a championship lifestyle.

Today's Agenda

Giving them a garland instead of ashes, the oil of gladness instead of mourning. The mantle of praise instead of a spirit of fainting, so they will be called oaks of righteousness, the planting of the Lord, that He may be glorified.
ISAIAH 61:3 NASB

Our days are hinged together in a unique way according to God's Word. Yesterdays pain, sorrow, and disappointment, as well as yesterdays victories and blessings, become todays agenda.

Were you rejected or alienated by someone yesterday? Then God's agenda for you today is one of restoration and reconciliation.

Were you struck with sickness or an injury yesterday? Then healing is on todays agenda.

Were you dealt a disappointment or handed a bad report? Then today is a day for hope and good news.

Were you struck with a calamity or disaster? Then today is the time for recovery and rejuvenation.

Did you fail in some way yesterday? Then Gods agenda for you today is a second chance!

No matter what worn-, frustration, or heartache you took with you to bed last night . . . today holds the hope tor a reversal of that "trouble." This is the redemptive nature of God's work in our lives: turning our losses into victories, our sorrow into gladness, and discouragement into reason for praise!

The prophet Isaiah tells us this process results in our becoming so firmly rooted in God's goodness we are like great "trees of righteousness." We grow to the point where we see no matter *what* may strike us on one day, the Lord has a plan for full recovery *and more* beginning the next. The apostle Paul echoed this when he wrote to the Romans:

"All things work together for good to those who love God, to those who are the called according to His purpose."
R O M A N S   8 : 2 8   N K J V

Our rebound is never back to the point where we began, but always takes us higher. We are wiser and richer. No matter what hits us, our roots grow deeper, our branches grow longer, and our fruit is increased.

Expect Gods turnabout in your life today!

———————————————

The Morning Hour

Be still, and know that I am God; I will be exalted among the nations, I will be exalted in the earth.
P S A L M   4 6 : 1 0   N K J V

So many of us find the mornings to be a time of "rushing." Various family members scurry in different directions with different needs and different timetables. One has lost a sock, another can't find last nights homework. One needs a sack lunch, another needs lunch money. One leaves with a kiss, another with a shout, and another needs encouragement to open her eyes as she stumbles out the door.

In sharp contrast stands the age-old advice that we each need a "quiet time" in the morning to center ourselves and to renew our relationship with our Heavenly Father. Carving out that time for yourself may be your supreme challenge of the day, but it is an effort worth its weight in gold, as so aptly stated by Bruce Fogarty:

THE MORNING HOUR

Alone with God, in quiet peace.
From earthly cares I find release;
New strength I borrow for each day
As there with God, I stop to pray.

Alone with God, my sins confess'd
He speaks in mercy, I am blest.
I know the kiss of pardon free,
I talk to God, He talks to me.

Alone with God, my vision clears
I see my guilt, the wasted years
I plead for grace to walk His way
And live for Him, from day to day.

Alone with God no sin between
His lovely lace so plainly seen;
My guilt all gone, my heart at rest
With Christ, my Lord, my soul is blest.

Lord, keep my life alone for Thee;
From sin and self Lord, set me free.
And when no more this earth I trod
They'll say, "He walked alone with God."[29]

Stay the Course

He [Jesus] steadfastly set his face to go to Jerusalem.
L U K E   9 : 5 1   K J V

The Saturday of the dog sled derby dawned as a bright, clear, cold winter morning. The people of the small Wisconsin town on the southern shore of Lake Superior looked forward to the annual competition. The one-mile course across the ice had been marked out by little fir trees set into the surface of the frozen lake. Spectators standing on the steep slope along the shore had a good view of the entire course.

The contestants were all children—ranging from large, older boys with several dogs and big sleds to one little guy who appeared to be no more than live years old. He entered the race with a little sled pulled by his small dog and lined up with the rest of the entrants waiting for the race to begin.

When the signal was sounded declaring the start of the race, the racers took off in a flurry and the youngest contestant with his little dog was quickly outdistanced. In fact, the larger and more experienced racers disappeared so quickly down the course that the little guy was hardly in the race at all. The contest was going well, however, and even though in last place, the little fellow stayed in the competition, enjoying every minute.

About halfway around the course, the dog team that was in second began to overtake the team that was in the lead. The dogs came too close to the lead team and soon the two teams were in a fight. Then, as each sled reached the fighting, snarling animals, they joined in the fracas.

None of the drivers seemed to be able to steer their teams clear of the growling brawl, and soon all of the dogs and racers became one big seething mass of kids, sleds, and dogs — all that is, but the little fellow and his one dog. He managed to stay the course and was the only one to finish the race.[30]

Each day holds the potential for something to sidetrack us from our intended purpose. No matter how great the distraction, we can finish the course if we stay focused and keep going!

———————————

Prepare to Dare

Every prudent man acts out of knowledge, but a fool exposes his folly.
PROVERBS 13:16

Trying something new can be lightening, and may even be dangerous. That's why its much smarter to take a calculated risk than a reckless plunge.

A calculated risk is what Charles Lindbergh took when he decided to fly across the Atlantic, alone, in a single-engine plane. Was Lindbergh fearful? He certainly might have been if he had never flown before, or if he had known nothing about planes. If he hadn't trusted the builder of his plane or his mechanics, he also would have had a good reason to be anxious. And if he had decided to make the trip on a whim, without advance planning, he certainly would have been labeled foolish.

But none of those factors were true in Lindberghs case. He was an experienced pilot and mechanic who personally spent months overseeing the construction of his plane. He participated in the planning of every detail of his historic flight. The end result was a safe trip, finished ahead of schedule with fuel to spare.[31]

To a great extent, "Lucky Lindy" made his own luck.

Likewise, heroic spiritual moments are nearly always grounded in advance preparation. Moses grew up in Pharaohs court, unknowingly being prepared for the day he would demand that Pharaoh let his people leave Egypt. Daniel was a man of prayer years before the king issued a decree banning prayer. The violation landed Daniel in a lion's den, where his prayers of protection were answered.

David was part of Saul's royal court and married to Saul's daughter. This was part of his preparation for assuming the throne one day. The years he spent in the wilderness prepared him spiritually to trust God, and God alone, to preserve him, protect him, and help him rule an empire. Esther prepared herself for a year before she won the "contest" to be queen. She prepared herself again before boldly coming to the king to expose the enemy of her people.

You may not see clearly what God's purpose is for your life, but you can trust in the fact He is preparing you for it. He will not waste a moment of your life. So make every relationship and experience count today, knowing He is grooming you for greatness!

What Are You Doing Today?

Praise the Lord, all you Gentiles! Laud Him, all you peoples!
For His merciful kindness is great toward us. And the truth
of the Lord endures forever.
PSALM 117:1-2 NKJV

In the Middle Ages a man was sent to a building site in France to see how the workers fell about their labor. He approached the first worker and asked, "What are you doing?"

The worker snapped at him, "Are you blind? I'm cutting these impossible boulders with primitive tools and putting them together the way the boss tells me. I'm sweating under this hot sun. My back is breaking. I'm bored. I make next to nothing!"

The man quickly backed away and found a second worker, to whom he asked the same question, "What are you doing?"

The second worker replied, "I'm shaping these boulders into useable forms. Then they are put together according to the architects plans. I earn five francs a week and that supports my wife and family. It's a job. Could be worse."

A little encouraged but not overwhelmed by this response, the man went to yet a third worker. "What are you doing?" he asked.

"Why, can't you see?" the worker said as he lifted his arm to the sky. I'm building a cathedral!"[32]

How do you see *your* work today? Do you see it as drudgery without reward or purpose? Do you see it as "just a job"? Or, do you see your work as part of Gods master design, not only for you but for others? Do you see yourself as a partner with Him in establishing *His* kingdom on the earth?

How we regard our work may not effect whether a task gets done or not. It will, however, have an impact on the quality of our work and our productivity. The real impact of how we led about a job lies in this: the more positive we *feel* about our work, the greater the satisfaction we have at day's end, and the less damaging stress we internalize. Those who see value in their jobs enjoy a greater sense of purpose.

Any job can be done with grace, dignity, style, and purpose . . . you only have to choose to see it that way!

––––––––––––––––––––––––––––

Soul Shower

Create in me a clean heart, O God.
PSALM 51:10 NKJV

Much of our morning routine is spent getting clean—taking a bath or shower, washing our hair, and brushing our teeth. But how much time and attention do we give to cleaning our heart? Don't forget to ask God to create a clean heart in you today!

Generous in love – God, give grace!
Huge in mercy – wipe out my bad record.
Scrub away my guilt, soak out my sins in your laundry.
I know how bad I've been; my sins are staring me down.
You're the One I've violated, and you've seen it all,
seen the full extent of my evil.
You have all the facts before you;
whatever you decide about me is fair.
I've been out of step with you for a long time . . .
What you're after is truth from the inside out.
Enter me, then; conceive a new, true life.
Soak me in your laundry and I'll come out clean,

scrub me and I'll have a snow-white life.
Tune me in to foot-tapping songs,
set these once-broken bones to dancing.
Don't look too close for blemishes,
give me a clean bill of health.
God, make a fresh start in me,
shape a Genesis week from the chaos of my life.
Don't throw me out with the trash.
or fail to breathe holiness in me.
Bring me back from gray exile,
put a fresh wind in mv sails!
Give me a job teaching rebels your ways
so the lost can find their way home.
Commute mv death sentence, God,
my salvation God. and I'll sing anthems to your
life-giving ways.
Unbutton my lips, dear God;
I'll let loose with your praise.

   P S A L M   5 1 ,   T H E   M E S S A G E[33]

_____

Reciprocity

Pray for each other so that you max he healed.
J A M E S   5 : 1 0

Sometimes when we focus on helping others, we end up solving our own problems. That certainly was true for David, an eight-year-old from Wisconsin who had a speech impediment. His problem made him hesitant to read aloud or speak up in class.

Davids mother also had a problem—multiple sclerosis. One winter day she and David were out walking and her cane slipped on an icy patch, causing her to fall. She was unhurt, but the incident left David wishing he could do something to help her.

Some time later, David's teacher assigned her students to come up with an invention for a national contest. He decided he would invent a cane that wouldn't slide on ice by putting a nail on the bottom of it. After his mother expressed concern about the nail damaging floor coverings, he developed a retractable system. Much like a ball-point pen, the nail could be popped out of sight by releasing a button at the top of the cane.

David's invention earned him first prize in the contest. As the winner, he was required to make public appearances and communicate with those who expressed an interest in his project. The more he talked about the cane, the less noticeable his speech impediment became![34]

Who needs your help today?

They may not need you to invent something for them. They may simply need your assistance on a project, a word of encouragement, or prayer for a particular need. You will find, as you extend the effort, time, and energy to help someone, something inside you will be softened, healed, renewed, or strengthened. An outward expression toward others always does something inwardly that enables, empowers, and enhances the character of Christ Jesus in us.

That's God's principle of reciprocity!

———————————————

At Last . . .

I will praise You, for You have answered me, and have become my salvation.
P S A L M   1 1 8 : 2 1   N K J V

The story is told of a diamond prospector in Venezuela named Rafael Solano. He was one of many impoverished natives and fortune seekers who came to sift through the rocks of a dried-up riverbed reputed to have diamonds. No one, however, had had any luck for some time in finding any diamonds in the sand and pebbles. One by one, those who came left the site—their dreams shattered and their bodies drained.

Discouraged and exhausted, Solano had just about decided it was time for him to give up too. He had nothing to show for months of hard work.

Then Solano stooped down one last time and scooped up a handful of pebbles, if only so he could say he had personally inspected every pebble in his claim. From the pebbles in his hand, he pulled out one that seemed a little different. He weighed it in his other hand. It seemed heavy. He measured it and weighed it on a scale. Could it be?

Sure enough, Solano had found a diamond in the rough! New York jewelry dealer Harry Winston paid Solano $200,000 for that stone. When it was cut and polished, it became known as the Liberator, and it is considered the largest and purest unmined diamond in the world.

You may have been plugging away at a project for weeks, even months or years, without seeing much progress. Today may be the day. Don't give up!

The Scriptures are filled with examples of men and women who, on the verge of disaster or failure, experienced God's creative work in their lives. Remind yourself . . .

- *God's Word is true.*
- *God can part the sea.*
- *God can heal the incurable.*
- *God can provide water from a rock and manna in the wilderness.*
- *God can conquer your enemies.*
- *God can still deliver from the fiery furnace and the lion's den.*

Persevere in what He has asked you to do today, because your rewards will be more than you can think or imagine!

———————————————

Forgiveness

Forgive us our debts, as we also have forgiven our debtors.
MATTHEW 6:12

———————————————

I t's hard to start the day when you are still carrying around a hurt you have not forgiven. One morning Denise Stovall's daughter, Deanna, taught her a special lesson about forgiveness.

"Mama! How do you spell 'Louis'?" Deanna asked as she rushed into the kitchen.

"Louis? Who's Louis?" asked Denise.

"You know," said the five-year-old. "He's the boy who gave me my black eye."

For several days Denise had asked herself how a child could be so mean to another child. Anger sizzled inside her every time she saw the black and blue mark around Deannas bright, hazel eye. Slamming the oven door closed as if it were the person in question, she said, "Why on earth do you want to know how to spell his name — especially after what he did to you?"

Deanna's reply reminded Denise of why Jesus said, "Let the little children come unto me, for of such is the kingdom of Heaven."

"W-e-l-l, at church yesterday, Miss Mae told us we should make paper chains for All Saints Day. She said to make a ring every time somebody does a nice thing like Jesus did, and then put that persons name on the ring. Louis told me on the bus today that he was sorry he hit me in my eye, and that was nice. I want to put his name on this ring and make it part of the chain, so we can pray for him so he won't do it again."

As Denise stood in the middle of the kitchen with her hands on her hips, the words of a recent sermon came back to convict her: "Forgiveness, no matter how long it takes or how difficult it is to attain, is the only path to healing and freedom."

Upon reflection, Denise thought Deanna's bruised eyelid looked just a *little* better.

Before you start the day, make certain you are free from all unforgiveness and offense. Remember how much God has forgiven you, and it will be easier to forgive others!

———————————————

Invited to Breakfast

You, O Lord, . . . know the hearts of all.
ACTS 1:24 NKJV

———————————

Most people wake up to an alarm clock ringing at an appointed hour rather than to a rooster crowing in the barnyard. But for the apostle Peter, the crowing rooster on the early morning of Jesus' crucifixion was a "wake-up call"—it woke him up to who he really was. In Peters worst moment he had denied knowing his friend and teacher, Jesus. He wept bitterly over his betrayal, and must have felt terrible guilt and shame afterward.

Then one morning after His resurrection, Jesus appeared to the disciples, who were fishing at the Sea of Tiberias. He called out from the shore and asked if they had caught any fish. The disciples didn't recognize Him and called back, "No." Jesus told them to throw the net on the other side of the boat, and the catch was so great they were unable to haul it in. Now they knew the man directing them was Jesus and headed to shore.

When the disciples got there, Jesus invited them to eat with Him. "Come and have breakfast," He said. In the dawning hours of the day, the resurrected Jesus cooked breakfast for them.

How do you think Peter felt when, after the greatest failure of his life, Jesus wanted to spend time with him, eat with him, and even help him fish? Jesus sought out the disciple who had let Him down when He needed him most. Moreover, He called Peter to lead His followers.

Like Peter, there are experiences in our days that serve as "wake-up calls" to who we claim to be. Those "wake-up calls" come in the form of opportunities to compromise who we are and what we believe. How do we act when others aren't around? How do we handle situations that can violate our integrity? To live a compromised life is to deny Jesus—the same as Peter did. (See Titus 1:16.)

It is always important for us to spend time with the Lord, but when we need to come clean in our heart, it is especially important. Jesus always invites us to fellowship with Him. He always forgives.

Whatever mistakes or compromises we made yesterday, Jesus still loves us today and says, "Come and have breakfast with Me."

Selling Things Right

If we confess our sins, he is faithful and just and will forgive us our sins and purify us from all unrighteousness.
1 JOHN 1:9

———————————————

Bruce Catton was a great Civil War historian who wrote numerous well-known books, including *A Stillness at Appomattox*. In the opinion of former Congressman and US ambassador Fred J. Eckert, Catton had a wonderful way of dealing with his errors.

It seems that when Eckert was a high-school sophomore, he read one of Catton's books, *This Hallowed Ground*. Moved by it, he sought out other books on the Civil War. In one, he discovered Catton had made a mistake in *This Hallowed Ground*. He had transposed the names of a first and second officer.

Eckert's teacher encouraged him to write Catton about the mistake. When he did, Catton responded by sending him autographed copies of several of his books, including a copy of *This Hallowed Ground*. In it he wrote, "To Fred Eckert, who caught me napping at Fort Donelson."

Eckert says he learned a valuable lesson from this experience: If you always do your best, you probably won't make too many serious errors. And when you do slip up from time to time, the best thing to do is acknowledge it and move on.[35]

Many of us spend a great deal of time and effort justifying or covering our sins and mistakes. The truth is, it is much easier to confess those sins, ask God's forgiveness, seek the forgiveness of others involved, and then move forward.

It is human pride that hinders us from acknowledging our mistakes, and perhaps that is the reason pride is considered the chief of all sins. It keeps us from repentance, which cuts off our intimacy with God.

Start your day with a clean slate. Ask the Lord to forgive you of all that is left unforgiven. Accept His forgiveness. Make amends as may be needed. And then get on with the business of living the life the Lord has called you to!

———————————————

A Soaring Imagination

Faith is the substance of things hoped for, the evidence of things not seen.
HEBREWS 11:1 NKJV

In his classic self-help book *Think & Grow Rich,* Napoleon Hill wrote, "Whatever the mind of man can conceive and believe, he can achieve." His premise, and that of many others, is that once the human mind has been programmed with a certain expectation, it will begin to act to fulfill that expectation.

The Scriptures declared this principle long before Hill wrote his book. Faith is believing and then seeing. It is expecting a miracle before receiving a miracle.

The Aluminum Company of America coined an interesting word: imagineering. They combined the idea of imagining a product or service, with the idea that this dream could then be engineered into a reality. Throughout history we've seen this principle at work.

- *A primitive ancestor came up with the idea that it was easier to roll objects than drag them — and he carved a wheel from stone.*

- *A man named Gutenberg imagined that letters might be set in metal and combined to create words, which then could be printed repeatedly with the application of ink. He set about to make such a machine.*

- *Men designed cathedrals that took decades to build — but build them they did.*

Your future will be impacted directly by the *ideas* and *dreams* that you have today. What you begin to believe for, and then how you act on that belief, will result in what you have, do, and are in the days, weeks, months, and years ahead.

Let your "faith imagination" soar today. Believe for Gods highest and best in your life. And then begin to live and work as if that miracle is on its way.

———————————————

Always There

Thou wilt keep him in perfect peace, whose mind is stayed on thee: because he trusteth in thee.
ISAIAH 26:3 KJV

A businessman once said: "Sometimes, after waking in the morning, I am appalled by the thought of all the duties and appointments that await me in the next eight or ten hours.

"Then I repeat to myself the words: 'In quietness and confidence shall be thy strength;' and 'Thou wilt keep him in perfect peace, whose mind is stayed on thee.' It is astonishing how quickly the load is lifted once I remind myself of God's presence and help. The strain and tension disappear and in its place a feeling of serenity and peace wells up within me."

Dr. Frank Laubach learned to be aware of the presence of God by disciplining his thoughts to think on God once every minute. He called it "the game of the minutes." Jacob Boehm, a sixteenth-century saint, also spoke of a practice that involved an almost continual awareness of God's presence: "If Thou dost once every hour throw thyself . . . into the abysmal mercy of God, then Thou shalt receive power to rule over death and sin."

The airplane pilot radios a message to a control tower every hour and receives an answer. Thus he keeps "on the beam." He is in touch with the controller, he receives his orders, and reports his position. He knows if the station does not hear from him at the appointed time, they will be alerted to the fact he and his passengers may be in danger.

Not everyone has Laubach's or Boehm's discipline. But wouldn't it be reassuring to talk to and hear from the control tower at least every hour during the day? It is as simple as uttering a prayer or repeating a scripture—"Thou wilt keep me in perfect peace."

The Value of One

*There is joy in the presence of the angels of God over one
sinner who repents.*
LUKE 15:10 NASB

Some days its hard just to get out of bed. Our motivation is fading or completely gone. We are overcome with a "What difference does it make?" attitude. We become overwhelmed at the enormity of the duties before us. Our talents and resources seem minuscule in comparison to the task.

A businessman and his wife once took a much-needed getaway at an oceanside hotel. During their stay a powerful storm arose, lashing the beach and sending massive breakers against the shore. The storm woke the man. He lay still in bed listening to the storms fury and reflecting on his own life of constant and continual demands and pressures.

Before daybreak the wind subsided. The man got out of bed to go outside and survey the damage done by the storm. He walked along the beach and noticed it was covered with starfish that had been thrown ashore by the massive waves. They laid helpless on the sandy beach. Unable to get to the water, the starfish faced inevitable death as the suns rays dried them out.

Down the beach a ways the man saw a figure walking along the shore. The figure would stoop and pick something up. In the dim of the early-morning twilight he couldn't quite make it all out. As he approached he realized it was a young boy picking up the starfish one at a time and flinging them back into the ocean to safety.

As the man neared the young boy he said, "Why are you doing that? One person will never make a difference—there are too many starfish to get back into the water before the sun comes up."

The boy said sadly, "Yes, that's true," and then bent to pick up another starfish. Then he said, "But I can sure make a difference to that one."

God never intended for an individual to solve all of life's problems. But He did intend for each one of us to use whatever resources and gifts He gave us to make a difference where we are.[36]

Serendipity Moments

We are his workmanship, created in Christ Jesus unto good works.
E P H E S I A N S   2 : 1 0   K J V

Serendipity, according to *Merriam-Websters Collegiate Dictionary*, is "the faculty or phenomenon of finding valuable or agreeable things not sought for." We sometimes call it an "accident, dumb luck, or fate," but serendipity has given us new products and better ways of doing things.

We all know examples of serendipity, such as Columbus' discovery of America while searching for a route to India. Maple syrup was discovered by Native Americans when, needing water, they tapped a maple tree and made the first maple syrup as they boiled off the sap. Westward-traveling pioneers looking for water stopped at a stream for a drink and found gold nuggets in the water.

While George Balias was driving his car through a car wash, he had a moment of serendipity that made him a millionaire. As he watched the strings of the brushes cleaning his car, he turned his mind to his list of things to do, among them edging his lawn.

Suddenly an idea "popped" into his head. He took another long look at the strings on the rotating brush. The strings straightened out when turning at high speed, but were still flexible enough to reach into every nook and cranny of his car to get it clean. He asked himself, *Why not use a nylon cord, whirling at high speed, to trim the grass and weeds around the trees and the house?* His idea—his serendipity—led to the invention of the Weedeater.

Where do we get new ideas? God is the Master behind serendipity! He may not always give you a million-dollar idea, but He will make you more creative. One expert gives this advice: Capture the ideas, jot them down quickly before they are gone, and evaluate later. Take time to daydream with the Lord. Seek new challenges. Expand your perspective. Learn and do new things.[37]

Remember today that God is your Creator—and the Creator of everything in the universe. Ask Him to inspire you with new ideas that can glorify Him and benefit others. We are co-creators with Him!

———————————————————

Who Says You Can't?

I can do all things through Christ who strengthens me.
PHILIPPIANS 4:13 NKJV

You can do anything. That's what Kent Cullers' parents told him as he was growing up. That's what many parents tell their children. But Cullers was born blind. Even so, if a child hears the phrase. *You can do anything,* often enough, it sinks in. It bears fruit. And it certainly did in Cullers' case.

As a young boy he insisted on climbing trees and riding a bicycle. His father arranged a job transfer to California so the boy could attend a regular school, and Cullers became a straight-A student. He was valedictorian of his high-school class and a National Merit Scholar. He went on to earn a Ph.D. in physics.

Cullers' first love has always been space, so it seems fitting that he found himself employed at NASA. As a researcher, one of his jobs was to design equipment to help scientists search for signs of intelligent communication in outer space.[38]

How does a blind man see what others can't? He uses his "mind's eye." He also uses his other senses—perhaps a little better than most people. Above all, he continues to tell himself what his parents taught him early in life: *You can do anything.*

The apostle Paul would have added a key phrase to Cullers' parental advice. *Through Christ who gives me strength.* The source of all our ability, energy, and creativity is the Lord Himself. It is He who challenges us to go forward and equips us to get the task done. It is the Lord working in us to enable us, working through us to empower us, and working on our behalf to enrich us.

At the same time, the Lord expects us to do two things: first, to open ourselves to His presence and power; and second, to gel in gear. He calls us to believe and do.

What are you believing today? What are you doing? Activate both your believing and doing, synchronize both with the will of God, and you can't help but be launched to a higher and better position.

———————————————————

Open Door to Your Goal

Therefore, as we have opportunity, let us do good to all.
GALATIANS 6:10 NKJV

_____

Edwin C. Barnes had a burning desire to become a business associate of the great inventor Thomas A. Edison. He didn't want to work *for* Edison, he wanted to work *with* him.

As a step toward making his dream come true, Barnes applied for a job at Edison's lab in New Jersey. He was hired as an office worker at a minimum salary — a far cry from a partnership. Months passed with no change in his status or his relationship with Edison. Most people would have given up, feeling their job was taking them nowhere. Barnes, however, stayed on board. He became thoroughly aware of the office environment and each person's job, and he sought out ways to make each person's work more pleasant and efficient. Above all, he remained open and optimistic. He saw all that he did as preparation for the day when he would become a partner with Edison in a joint venture.

The day came when Edison presented the Edison Dictating Machine to his sales staff. They didn't believe it would sell. Barnes, however, saw this awkward-looking machine as his opportunity! He approached Edison, announcing he'd like to sell the dictating device. Since no one else had showed any enthusiasm for it, Edison gave Barnes the chance. He granted him an exclusive contract to distribute and market the office machine throughout America. Barnes succeeded in his goal of working *with* the great inventor, and achieved his goal to be a success in business at the same time.

Do you have a goal in your mind or heart today? You can be certain you will reach it as you serve others and help them reach their goals. The help you offer to a family member, neighbor, co-worker, or employer today will come back to you in success tomorrow.

Opportunity may arrive in your life today in the disguise of misfortune, defeat, rejection, or failure. See beyond the problems to consider the possibilities. Step out to help someone overcome their difficulties and you will be overwhelmed by the good fortune God sends your way!

Procrastination Leads Nowhere

I will hasten and not delay to obey your commands.
P S A L M   1 1 9 : 6 0

Morning is a great time to make a list of "things to do" and plan the day. It's also the best time to tackle those tasks that are the most difficult or we like least. If we procrastinate as the day wears on, rationalization sets in and sometimes even the tasks we had considered to be the most important are left undone.

Here's a little poem just for those who struggle with procrastination:

HOW AND WHEN

We often greatly bothered
By two fussy little men,
Who sometimes block our pathway
Their names are How and When.

If we have a task or duty

Which we can put off a while,
And we do not go and do it
You should see those two rogues smile!

But there is a way to beat them,
And I will tell you how:
I you have a task or duty,
Do it well, and do it now.

UNKNOWN

As part of your morning prayer time, ask the Lord to help you to overcome any tendency to procrastinate and prioritize projects according to His plans and purposes.

Often we ask the Lord, "What do You want me to do?" but then fail to ask Him one of the key follow-up questions, "When do You want me to do this?" When we have a sense of Gods timing, and in some cases His urgency about a matter, our conviction grows to get the job done right away.

Gods "omnipresence" means He is always with you, and He is always "timely." He's with you in the "now" moments of your life. He is concerned with how you use every moment of your time. Recognize that He desires to be part of your time-management and task-completion process today!

Payoffs

The people did the work faithfully.
2 CHRONICLES 34:12 NRSV

Thomas Edison was once quoted as saying, "I am wondering what would have happened to me if some fluent talker had converted me to the theory of the eight-hour day, and convinced me that it was not fair to my fellow workers to put forth my best efforts in my work. I am glad that the eight-hour day had not been invented when I was a young man. II my life had been made up of eight-hour days, I do not believe I could have accomplished a great deal. This country would not amount to as much as it does if the young men had been afraid that they might earn more than they were paid."

Edison attributed his success to "two-percent inspiration and 98-percent perspiration."

Missionary and explorer David Livingston worked 12-hour days in a factory—from 6:00am to 8:00pm. When he got off work he attended night classes for two hours, and then went home to study late into the night.

Leonardo da Vinci, the great 15th-century Italian painter, sculptor, architect, engineer, and scientist, understood the need for hard work. He said, "Thou, Oh God, doth sell to us all good things at the price of labor. Work is the seed from which grows all good things you hope for."

Nature also provides a striking example of hard work. Honey bees collect nectar from 125 clover heads to make one gram of honey. That adds up to three million trips to make one pound of honey!

And Michelangelo, one of the greatest artists of all time, disputed the marvel of his own talent. "If people knew how hard I have had to work to gain my mastery, it wouldn't seem wonderful at all."

"Overnight" success, making it big, and "lucking out" often disguises hard work.

Thank God every morning that you have something to do which must be done, whether you like it or not. Then do it to the best of your ability.

———————————————————

Ultimate Victors

What shall we then say to these things? If God be for us, who can be against us?
ROMANS 8:31

D id you ever try to reroute a small stream by building a dam across the water with rocks and stones when you were a child? Did you ever build a mud dam to collect the flowing water and make a pool in which to sail your toy boat? Our childlike efforts were never completely successful, were they? The stones eventually gave way to the rush of water and the mud dam finally washed downstream.

For 5,000 years dams have been used to control water — to prevent floods, divert rivers, store water, and irrigate land. But even todays modern dams do not completely stop the flow of water back into the streams or prevent its eventual return to the oceans.

Every day we meet challenges that can potentially divert us and even temporarily defeat God's purpose for our life. Our life may have been derailed by failures, bad decisions, or mistakes, but if we give those circumstances to the Lord, they will never defeat His plan for us. In fact, we are usually in awe as He takes those circumstances and uses them to accomplish His good and eternal purpose. (See Romans 8:28.)

Gods plan can never be defeated—and that is good news for you today. God is in control, which means nothing can happen which will defeat Him, even the willful disobedience of one person or a group of people.

If that is true for the Sovereign of the Universe, it is also true for us—if our purposes are aligned with His. Even though God's will in our life be temporarily diverted by our sin or mistakes, by circumstances, or even by the harm someone else inflicts on us, we can never be ultimately defeated as long as we are cooperating with Him.[39]

———————————————————

A Cork's Influence

Let us behave decently, as in the daytime . . . clothe
yourselves with the Lord Jesus Christ.
R O M A N S   1 3 : 1 3 - 1 4

A tour group passed through a particular room in a factory. They viewed an elongated bar of steel, which weighed five hundred pounds, suspended vertically by a chain. Near it, an average-size cork was suspended by a silk thread.

"You will see something shortly which is seemingly impossible," said an attendant to the group of sightseers. "This cork is going to set this steel bar in motion!"

She took the cork in her hand, pulled it only slightly to the side of its original position, and released it. The cork swung gently against the steel bar, which remained motionless.

For ten minutes the cork, with pendulum-like regularity, struck the iron bar. Finally, the bar vibrated slightly. By the time the tour group passed through the room an hour later, the great bar was swinging like the pendulum of a clock!

Many of us feel we are not exerting a feathers weight of influence upon others or making a dent in the bastions of evil in the world. Not so! Sometimes we don't realize how powerful the cumulative influence of God's goodness which we walk in is to those around us.

Not everyone is called to spread the love of Jesus through the pulpit, on the evangelistic trail, or in a full-time counseling ministry. Most of us are called to live our lives as "corks," through word and example— quietly, gently tapping away through the work of our daily lives. Tap by loving tap, in God's time, even the quietest Christian can make a huge difference in the lives of those whom preachers may never reach.

One modern-day philosopher has estimated that the average person encounters at least twenty different people in the course of a day, with a minimum of eye contact and exchange of words or gesture. That's at least twenty opportunities for a cork to "tap" at the collective human heart.

As you go about your day, remember that even a smile can warm a strangers heart and draw them to Jesus.

References

Unless otherwise indicated, all Scripture quotations are taken from the *Holy Bible, New International Version®* NIV®. Copyright © 1973, 1978, 1984 by International Bible Society. Used by permission of Zondervan Publishing House. All rights reserved.

Scripture quotations marked NKJV are taken from *The New King James Version* of the Bible. Copyright © 1979, 1980, 1982, 1994 by Thomas Nelson, Inc., Publishers. Used by permission.

Scripture quotations marked NASB are taken from the *New American Standard Bible.* Copyright © 1960, 1962, 1963, 1968, 1971. 1972, 1973, 1975, 1977 by The Lockman Foundation. Used by permission.

Scripture quotations marked KJV are taken from the *King James Version* of the Bible.

Scripture quotations marked NRSV are taken from *The New Revised Standard Bible*, copyright © 1989 by the Division of Christian Eduction of the Churches of Christ in the United States of America and is used by permission.

Scripture quotations marked AMP are taken from *The Amplified Bible, Old Testament.* Copyright © 1965 by Zondervan Publishing House, Grand Rapids, Michigan. *New Testament* copyright © 1958 by The

Endnotes

1."Morning Has Broken," Eleanor Farjeon, *The United Methodist Hymnal*. (Nashville, TN: The United Methodist Publishing House, 1989), p. 145.

2."Introduction," Louise Haskins, *Traveling Toward Sunrise*, Mrs. Charles Cowman, ed. (Grand Rapids, Ml: Zondervan Publishing House, no pub date), p. 1.

3.*The New Dictionary of Thoughts*, Tryon Edwards, ed. (NY: Standard Book Company, 1963), p. 506.

4."Fill My Cup, Lord," Richard Blanchard, Chorus Book (Dallas, TX: Word, Inc., 1971).

5.*The Man Who Talks With the Flowers*, Glenn Clark (St. Paul: Macalester Park Publishing Co., 1939), pp. 17, 21-22.

6.*Book of Prayers*, Robert Van de Weyer, ed. (NY: Harper Collins, 1993). p. 67.

7.*Songs from the Land of Dawn*, Toyohiko Kagawa and other Japanese Poets, Lois J. Erickson, trans. (NY: Friendship Press, 1949), pp. 20-21.

8.*New Every Morning*, Philip E. Howard Jr. (Grand Rapids, MI: Zondervan, 1969), pp. 12-13.

9.*Decision*, February 1996, p. 25.

10.*Encyclopedia of Sermon Illustrations*, David F. Burgess (St. Louis, MO: Concordia Publishing House, 1988), p. 113.

11.*The Finishing Touch*, Charles Swindoll (Dallas: Word Publishing. 1994), p. 274.

12."Awake My Soul," Philip Doddridge, *Methodist Hymnal,* (Nashville, TN: United Methodist Publishing House, 1966), p. 249.

13.*Illustrations for Preaching and Teaching*, Craig B. Larson (Grand Rapids: Ml: Baker Book House Co., 1993), p. 36.

14.*The Family Book of Best Loved Poems*, David L. George, ed. (NY: Doubleday & Co., 1952), p. 63.

15.*The Open Door,* Helen Keller, (NY: Doubleday Sr Co., 1957), p. 12-13.

16.*Silent Strength for My Life*, Lloyd John Ogilvie (Eugene, OR: Harvest House Publishers, 1990), p. 32.

17."Lord of the Dance," Sydney Carter, *The United Methodist Hymnal.* (Nashville: The United Methodist Publishing House, 1989), p. 261.

18.*Legacy of a Pack Rat*, Ruth Bell Graham (Nashville: Thomas Nelson, 1989), p. 49.

19.*A Guide to Prayer*, Reuben P. Job and Norman Shawchuck (Nashville: The Upper Room, 1983), p. 234.

20.*The Harper Collins Book of Prayers*, Robert Van de Weyer, ed. (NY: Harper Collins, 1993), pp. 389-390.

21.*San Luis Obispo Telegraph-Tribune* January 31, 1996, B-3.

22.*Spiritual Disciplines for the Christian Life*, Donald S. Whitney (Colorado Springs: NavPress, 1991), p. 37.

23.*Pacific Discovery*, Spring 1994, p. 20.

24.*The Joy of Working*, Denis Waitley and Reni Witt (NY: Dodd Mead and Company, 1985), p. 253.

25.*A Guide to Prayer*, Reuben P. Job and Norman Shawchuck, (Nashville: The Upper Room, 1983), p. 177.

26.*Pacific Discovery*, Summer 1990, p. 23-24.

27.*A Guide to Prayer*, Reuben P. Job and Norman Shawchuck (Nashville: The Upper Room, 1983), p. 176.

28.*Reader's Digest*, October 1991, p. 59-62.

29.*Knight's Master Book of 4,000 Illustrations*, Walter B. Knight (Grand Rapids, Ml: William B. Eerdmans Publishing Co., 1956), p. 93.

30.*Illustrations Unlimited* James Hewett, ed. (Wheaton: Tyndale House, 1988), p. 159.

31.*Reader's Digest*, March 1991, p. 128-132.

32.*The Joy of Working*, Denis Waitley and Reni L. Witt (NY: Dodd, Mead and Company, 1985), p. 23-24.

33.*The Message*, Eugene H. Peterson (Colorado Springs: Navpress, 1993, 1994, 1995), pp. 722-723.

34.Gary Johnson, *Readers Digest*, September 1991, p. 164-165.

35.*Readers Digest*, September 1991, p. 115-116.

36.*The Finishing Touch*, Charles R. Swindoll (Dallas: Word Publishing, 1994), pp. 186-187.

37.*Readers Digest*, December 1992, pp. 101-104.

38.*Reader's Digest*, December 1991, p. 96-100.

39."Putting Away Childish Things," David Seamands, *The Inspirational Study Bible*, Max Lucado, gen. ed. (Dallas: Word Publishing, 1995), pp. 35-36.

Additional copies of this book and other titles in the
Quiet Moments with God series are available from your
local bookstore.

In the Kitchen with God
Coffee Break with God
Daybreak with God
In the Garden with God
Sunset with God
Tea Time with God
Through the Night with God
Christmas With God